GUIDE T
ALTERNATIVE INVESTMENT MARKET

EDGE & ELLISON

GUIDE TO THE ALTERNATIVE INVESTMENT MARKET

Brian Finch MA, MBA, FCCA
Management Consultant

Graham Woolfman BSc, FCA
Partner, Levy Gee, Chartered Accountants

Butterworths
London, Dublin and Edinburgh
1995

United Kingdom	Butterworths, a Division of Reed Elsevier (UK) Ltd Halsbury House, 35 Chancery Lane, LONDON WC2A 1EL and 4 Hill Street, EDINBURGH EH2 3JZ
Australia	Butterworths Pty Ltd, SYDNEY, MELBOURNE, BRISBANE, ADELAIDE, PERTH, CANBERRA and HOBART
Canada	Butterworths Canada Ltd, TORONTO and VANCOUVER
Ireland	Butterworth (Ireland) Ltd, DUBLIN
Malaysia	Malayan Law Journal Sdn Bhd, KUALA LUMPUR
New Zealand	Butterworths of New Zealand Ltd, WELLINGTON and AUCKLAND
Puerto Rico	Butterworths of Puerto Rico, Inc, SAN JUAN
Singapore	Reed Elsevier (Singapore) Pte Ltd, SINGAPORE
South Africa	Butterworths Publishers (Pty) Ltd, DURBAN
USA	Butterworth Legal Publishers, CARLSBAD, California, and SALEM, New Hampshire

A CIP catalogue record for this book is available from the British Library.

ISBN 0 406 05354 5

Typeset by Kerrypress Ltd, Luton, Bedfordshire.
Printed and bound in Great Britain by Antony Rowe Ltd, Chippenham, Wiltshire.

Preface

This book provides practical explanation of the rules, regulations and laws that will govern the Alternative Investment Market, opened under the aegis of the Stock Exchange on 19 June 1995. It is intended to be of use to a widely spread audience, from market professionals who may want to find the detail brought together in one source, to companies seeking to join the market and their advisers, as well as to students who may be interested to know more about its background and workings.

Peering dimly into the mist ahead, we are greatly excited by the potential for this new market which, we believe, will have the ability to provide much needed assistance to young and dynamic companies. It should provide access to finance at a reasonable price, at a critical time in their development, and visibility in financial markets. Many of them will grow rapidly, although some will inevitably fail, and we believe the market should provide highly profitable investment opportunities to those who are prepared to accept the higher risk of failure.

We have been fortunate in the number of people who have assisted us in the preparation of this book by freely giving their opinions and expertise. We would particularly like to thank all the companies whose shares currently trade under the Stock Exchange's Rule 4.2 for their responses to our questionnaire. We are also grateful to Charles Abrams of S J Berwin and Paul Belsman of Levy Gee. The wisdom that may be contained in these pages is due to the many people who have helped and any errors are entirely ours. The new Alternative Investment Market has just opened for business at the time we are completing this manuscript and its detailed working is still developing. Many of the details of how the market will operate will come from custom and practice that will evolve, particularly over the first year or two of operation. However, we have tried, where appropriate, to predict what we believe to be the likely developments, based on experience of other markets and following many discussions with market professionals. As someone once said, the most difficult thing to forecast is the future.

We have quoted in this book from the Rules of the London Stock Exchange, reproduced forms with their kind permission and extracted data from information published by them. Any errors or omissions are not the responsibility of the Exchange. We acknowledge that the Exchange is the proprietor of and beneficially entitled to the copyright and all other rights of a like nature conferred in the UK (and throughout the world) in the Rules and the forms.

Brian Finch
Graham Woolfman
July 1995

Contents

Introduction

THE ALTERNATIVE INVESTMENT MARKET (AIM)

The Alternative Investment Market (AIM) is a new UK second tier market which follows from the Unlisted Securities Market (USM), which is due to close at the end of 1996. It is expected that many companies will join whose shares currently trade outside the control of the Stock Exchange, on the so-called 4.2 Market, but AIM is not intended to have the same unregulated form. While being a part of the London Stock Exchange (the Exchange), AIM has its own management team – in contrast to the two previous second tier markets set up by the Exchange in London: the USM and Third Market. This innovation is expected to ensure there are people within The Exchange dedicated to its development and supporting its distinct identity.

AIM is intended for small, young and growing companies that do not want or are not able to join the main stock market over which The Exchange presides, often called the Official List. Companies will be attracted by the easier entry requirements and the lighter regulation compared with the Official List, which ought to make it less costly to enter as well as less costly to observe continuing obligations. In addition, there are considerable tax reliefs available to shareholders and particularly to director shareholders because shares traded on AIM will be treated as unquoted for tax purposes.

Comparisons with NASDAQ

If the new market is successful in attracting young, dynamic companies then AIM may develop such a strong identity that it will prove to be a long-term alternative to joining the Official List, rather than just a feeder to a main market. A suitable role model might be the American stock exchange called NASDAQ which was also established as an enterprise market. This has grown over 20 years to have 70% of the market capitalisation of the New York Stock Exchange, which is the largest exchange in the world. NASDAQ has also provided crucial funding for smaller, developing businesses in the USA and has been so effective that many foreign companies (particularly high technology stocks) have chosen to join it rather than their own national exchanges. AIM too has the potential to attract foreign companies to trade their shares in London just as the 'senior' market has with the London International Stock Exchange.

However, this vision of AIM attracting second market trading to London from other countries will require a great deal of work to achieve. At present The Exchange does not seem to see this as the priority, which we believe it must be eventually, if the market is to be a success. If it is to be successful, not only must AIM attract investors in the UK but also meet competition from other European second markets and it must meet the challenge of the proposed pan-European market (EASDAQ).

If NASDAQ is a role model for the success of AIM, then it must be noted that there are significant features of the American market for smaller companies that are absent in the UK and indeed in other European countries. In particular, there are far more investors in smaller companies in the USA than in the UK: NASDAQ had 500 market makers at the end of 1994, compared with around 57 on The London Stock Exchange. AIM is likely to start with two or three market makers. About 11m Americans own shares in companies listed on NASDAQ although institutional investors own some 44% of the shares by value[1] (by contrast the London Stock Exchange is dominated by institutions owning over 80% of the shares by value). Even in London, which is the predominant European financial centre, with a far greater concentration of financial institutions than elsewhere in Europe, the number of funds investing in smaller companies is no more than a few dozen. But it is individuals as well as institutions who are important to the development of a market. There has

---

[1] NASDAQ published data 1993

been an increase in the number of individual stock market investors in the UK in recent years as a result of government privatisation of nationalised industries. However, many of these investors seem to keep their shares rather than buying and selling them; in any case the share trading habit does not seem to have spread to the smaller company end of the market. The long-term trend has been a concentration of share ownership in the hands of a relatively small number of institutions that manage pension and insurance funds, as well as personal saving schemes.

If it is the number of active investors who create an active market then London, for all its size, may not have the critical mass to support a second market. It is the subsequent trading that is essential for a thriving stock market, rather than just the initial flotation. If the shares, after the initial flotation, are hard to buy or sell then the appetite for flotations themselves may be restricted. In addition, the difficulty of trading shares affects the multiple of profits at which they sell, which affects the cost of raising funds through this market. It may also affect the ability of AIM companies to raise further funds through subsequent share offerings. Market insiders believe that shares trading on the 4.2 Market do so at a discount of around 20% to the price they would command on the Official List and there has been some research that seems to support this view. This discount may be a direct result of the greater difficulty in trading shares on the 4.2 Market.

We believe that AIM has the potential to be a great success but this will depend critically on the ability of its management to attract wide enough investor interest to achieve critical mass. If this critical mass cannot be achieved in the UK, then it will be necessary to look further afield to continental investors, whether through determined marketing, a merger of European second markets or the establishment of a European wide market (see **14.5.2**).

The Exchange is confident that most shares traded under Rule 4.2 will transfer to AIM, that some USM and even Official List shares will do so and that the market will attract many new entrants. It hopes to see over 200 shares trading on AIM within the next two to three years. Trading under Rule 4.2 will cease at the end of September 1995 and the companies currently using it will have limited choices if they want to provide a facility for shareholders to trade shares. Our research shows that while a number probably will not join AIM, the majority will – giving a considerable boost to the new market. Continued success of the new market will depend upon the confidence that can be generated as it develops. Previous experience with second tier markets has shown that this can fluctuate over time. We believe that the way AIM and its management have been established gives a good probability of sustainable success over the long term and that the targets that The Exchange has set are achievable.

KEY FEATURES OF AIM

The key features of AIM are as follows:

- AIM will provide companies with the ability to trade shares and to raise new finance.
- The Exchange sees AIM as a cheaper, less complicated option than full listing. The consensus from corporate advisers is that entry costs for companies seeking to raise new funds, may be 30 to 50% lower than for the Official List.
- AIM is primarily designed for young and growing companies which do not want or are not able to obtain a full listing.
- There are no eligibility criteria for new entrants to AIM, whether in size, profitability or length of track record.
- There are no Stock Exchange requirements for the percentage of shares in public hands or the number of shareholders.
- AIM will have lighter regulation than the Official List and investors will have to rely to a greater extent on their own judgement.
- Companies must have, at all times, an approved adviser to give guidance and a broker to act as a point of contact and to support trading.
- There will be fewer obligations for AIM companies to issue shareholder circulars: public announcements will be sufficient. This will make continuing costs for companies growing by acquisition or for those engaged in transactions with directors considerably lighter.
- AIM securities will be subject to The Exchange's Market Supervision and Surveillance Departments in the same way as the Official List.
- The Treasury announcement that AIM shares will be treated as unquoted for tax purposes will make it a very attractive market for many investors and particularly for shareholder directors.

- Documents produced for admission to AIM are the responsibility of the directors of the applicant and are not reviewed by the Exchange. The law clearly places responsibility on the directors for prospectuses issued to raise funds from the public.
- There is a prospect of AIM developing to offer an alternative to the Official List rather than just a stepping stone to it. This depends on attracting sufficient private and institutional investors to maintain a healthy trade in shares after they have been floated.

WHY INVEST IN SMALLER COMPANIES?

A very good reason for investing in smaller companies is that investment returns – on a portfolio basis – are higher. Over the long term, investment in smaller quoted companies has shown better returns than investment in the FTSE All Share Index (All Share). Evidence for this is provided by the performance of Hoare Govett's HG 1000 Index. Hoare Govett securities has sponsored and published work on a smaller companies index produced by Professors Dimson and Marsh from the London Business School. They established an index of the 1,000 smallest companies on the London Stock Exchange Official List in 1993 and 1994. These turned out to have a maximum market capitalisation of £50m and, in aggregate, accounted for some 2.5% of the total market capitalisation of the London Stock Market. Comparing the performance of this index with the All Share has shown that 'Over the long term, these minnows of the stock market have performed extremely well'[2]. The result, taken over a period from 1955 to 1993, was that the average annual return[3] on the HG 1000 was 24.7% and on the All Share 18.0%. This difference is very significant since, over a 20-year period, it would result in an investment of £1,000 in the HG 1000 having grown to be worth £82,666 while £1,000 on the All Share would only be worth £27,393. The smaller companies have not outperformed in each year throughout the period, but the periods of under performance have generally been short. From the beginning of 1989

---

[2] Dimson and Marsh 1995

[3] Note that it is assumed that dividends are reinvested. This is particularly important because a large proportion of the investment return is due to dividends rather than capital appreciation. Note also that taxation on dividends has not been taken into account.

to the end of 1992, the smaller companies underperformed the All Share, but 1993 and 1994 have seen a return to outperformance.

Investors are concerned both with the risk as well as the return on their investment. Risk is the possibility (or statistical probability) of losing their capital or of not achieving their target rate of return. The figures quoted above take the element of risk into account, in that they are averaged over 1,000 companies. During each year some of those companies will fail but overall the successes have balanced the failures and the result is the average annual 24.7% return over the period. It must be noted, however, that not all investors will have been able to spread their risk over a large number of investments and some investors will have lost money through investing in particular smaller companies. The Stock Exchange sees AIM as a higher risk market, though one that carries the potential for high returns. In fact the volatility, or variability, of annual returns from the smaller companies has been lower than the FTSE index but does seem to have converged towards it.

Clearly the performance of companies on AIM may prove to be very different from the HG 1000 since its make up is likely to be different. The smaller companies on the Official List include a number of potential recovery stocks that have underperformed and fallen in value. Such companies occasionally show spectacular recoveries. Others have been acquired by ambitious people to gain a Stock Exchange listing and access to equity funding, new businesses have been added and often the original business has been sold and the new concern has shown dramatic increases in value. At least in the first two or three years of its existence AIM is unlikely to have companies whose shares trade through it that have had the time to fall into either the category of the recovery vehicle or of the empty shell. However, Dimson and Marsh's research shows that dividend income greatly outweighs capital gains as a driver of overall investment returns on both the FTSE and HG 1000, which suggests that such sudden stars are unlikely to distort the picture provided by the long-term success of the 'minnows'.

The shares in smaller companies trading on the Official List, the USM and those trading under Rule 4.2 have been less easily traded than those of larger companies. The difference appears to be directly related to the size of the company. It appears also to be accounted for by sporadic trading rather than simply a consistently lower volume. This suggests that while it may take more time to effect a trade it should not be impossible to achieve a transaction except in very large quantities of stock. Indeed there are a number of institutions that have established, or are considering establishing, funds specialising in smaller companies. If the publicity for the new market is supported by new funds, brokers' analysis and investor newsletters then investor interest may become self-sustaining at a higher level of activity than has been seen previously in smaller company shares.

If a company has a good story to tell, is active in promoting itself and has good management then (subject to having released a sufficient proportion of its shares for trading) it should find an active market for its shares. On the other hand, a dull but worthy company is likely to find it hard to achieve an active market.

OUTLINE

This book comprises three parts: the background to AIM, the regulations applying to it, and practical issues of whether and how to join.

In Part One we set the scene to the London Stock Market itself, including a brief history of it and of the smaller company markets it has supported. This sets AIM in its context and attempts to develop some lessons from past experiences. While not wishing to provide a textbook of the detailed workings of the securities markets we do feel it is useful to summarise the key trading systems and the regulation of the market.

Part Two of the book is a guide to the regulations which explains the practical operation of the rules, regulations and codes of practice that govern AIM. This section is largely based upon the Rules of AIM published by The Stock Exchange and is supplemented by discussions we have had with The Exchange and with observers of the markets. We also refer to relevant legal sources on insider dealing and various codes of practice, where appropriate.

Finally, in Part Three, we deal with practical issues of alternatives to AIM, how to join AIM and how much it will cost, a discussion of who will be the investors in the market, and what tax reliefs may be available to them.

PART ONE

Background to AIM

CHAPTER 1

Background to the stock market

This chapter briefly summarises the history of The London Stock Exchange and summarises some of its key functions in order to set the scene for a discussion of second tier markets. We then describe the predecessors to AIM: the USM and the Third Market. Against this background it is easier to understand the differences between AIM and its predecessors and the stronger base on which it is built.

1.1 HISTORY OF THE LONDON STOCK EXCHANGE

The idea of a stock exchange grows naturally from that of joint stock companies, of which the first was founded in London in 1553. It was set up by a group of London merchants whose purpose was to search for a sea passage to the north of Russia, enabling trade to take place with the Far East without the long journey around Africa. A joint stock company is one where investors subscribe to ownership of units of equal value in a venture; these units are called shares. The natural progression from a certificate that proclaims ownership of a unit is that the owner may sell the unit. Soon this concept results in a market in such investments, with some middlemen acting as intermediaries between buyers and sellers. Once these intermediaries trade on their own account as well as on behalf of clients, the idea of a market maker is born.

By the mid-eighteenth century there was an active market in such shares. The trade took place informally around the coffee houses of the City.

Eventually one location predominated and the traders set up a membership, which acquired premises, moved and named their building The Stock Exchange.

An Exchange committee was set up and established rules. The number and value of joint stock companies grew, with funding for growing companies being sought from outside the small circle of London merchants. Whereas the market had originally operated essentially as a means for merchants to trade their investments it became, during the nineteenth century, more of a vehicle for this wider shareholding public that financed the growth in corporate enterprise.

During the nineteenth century and right up until 1973, there were many regional stock exchanges in the UK as well as The London Exchange. It was only in 1973 that all these regional exchanges finally merged.

1.1.1 Big Bang

In 1986 there occurred a series of significant changes to The Stock Exchange which became known as Big Bang, because they all happened at once:

1. Control of member firms, which previously had to be in the hands of individual members, was opened up to outside companies. This change was designed to give member firms access to larger amounts of capital in order to compete internationally.
2. The system of minimum commission levels set by the Exchange was abolished as a result of an out of court settlement with the government which had brought a case through the Restrictive Practices Court. This opened up the market for members to compete on price.
3. The separation of jobbing and broking was abolished. All firms became broker/dealers, able to act for clients or on their own account and also able to act as market makers.
4. The SEAQ (Stock Exchange Automated Quote) computer based quotation system was introduced at the same time, partly in order to support the other changes. It led to the end of the main trading floor of The Exchange, with dealing being conducted by telephone and computer links from many offices in the City of London and outside.

The impact of these changes was dramatic, with ownership of brokers transferring to major international banks and brokers. The market became more transparent, with dealing and settlement becoming faster, cheaper and more efficient.

1.2 SUMMARY OF THE LONDON STOCK EXCHANGE

The London Stock Exchange provides a convenient and regulated environment for trading in companies' securities. It also provides a system for the settlement of transactions (Talisman), methods for publicising share prices (SEAQ and a system for companies on the Official List which have less than two market makers (SEATS) – recently replaced with an upgraded SEATS PLUS) and an official company news service (RNS). It is not the only possible means for trading shares; at its simplest two individuals who happen to meet, one wanting to sell and one to buy, can carry out the transaction themselves, without needing a stock exchange. Other companies have also sought approval from the Securities and Investments Board, under the Financial Services Act, to carry on business as a recognised stock exchange.

The Exchange provides four different markets:

- UK and Irish equities;
- overseas equities;
- UK gilts;
- bonds and fixed interest stocks.

The new Alternative Investment Market is likely to trade predominantly in equities, but there is no reason why preference shares, debentures, warrants etc should not be traded on AIM.

Figure 1.1 below shows the distribution, by value, of securities between the Stock Exchange markets.

1.2.1 UK and Irish equities

At the end of 1994 The London Stock Exchange offered trading facilities in 2,070 UK and Irish companies as well as a further 207 USM companies all of which had an aggregate market value of nearly £780 bn. On this measure it is the third largest stock market in the world, after New York and Tokyo.

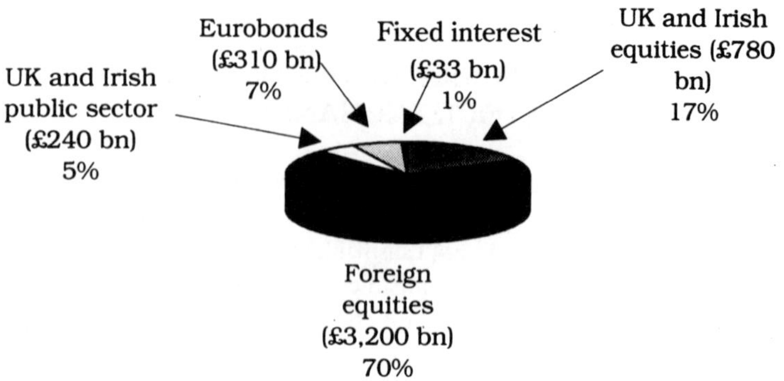

Figure 1.1: Distribution, by value, of securities between the Stock Exchange markets
Source: London Stock Exchange Fact Book 1994

1.2.2 Foreign equities

At the end of 1994 there were 464 foreign companies listed, having an aggregate market value of nearly £2,000 bn. This is the largest truly international stock exchange in the world by a substantial margin. These securities trade through a segment of the SEAQ system called SEAQ International that operates by slightly amended rules that are suited to international trading. There are, in turn, a number of country segments of SEAQ International.

In 1994 The Exchange launched its system of Global Depository Receipts (GDR) for the trading of securities in foreign companies. A GDR is a negotiable certificate which is evidence of the ownership of the underlying securities that are held in a bank or similar institution. They may offer advantages over trading the underlying shares because of national restrictions on foreign ownership, foreign exchange issues or simply make settlement easier. Already GDRs are traded in 90 foreign companies out of the total of over 900 foreign companies traded on SEAQ International.

AIM will also be open to foreign companies and GDRs would, in principle, be acceptable as securities to be traded through it.

The business of The Exchange in both UK and foreign securities has shown continued rapid growth over many years. As illustrated in Figure 1.2 below, the dramatic rise in volume and value of trading during 1987 was the exception to the long-term trend which was corrected by the crash in values and volumes of trading that occurred towards the end of that year.

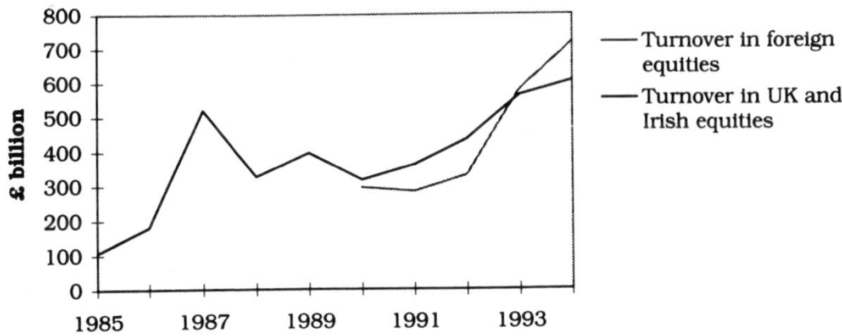

Figure 1.2: Annual turnover in equities on the London Stock Exchange
Source: London Stock Exchange Fact Book 1994

The turnover in London of foreign equities is now higher than that of UK equities, reinforcing London's reputation as the premier international exchange. Table 1.1 shows the breakdown of the £720 bn turnover in foreign equities transacted via London in 1994, between the most important countries.

Japan	23%
France	14%
Germany	11%
Netherlands	8%
Switzerland	7%
	63%

Table 1.1: Turnover in London of foreign equities
Source: London Stock Exchange Fact Book 1994

Based on their own listed equities, The London Stock Exchange appears to be third in size, a long way behind the New York and Tokyo stock exchanges (see Table 1.2 below). However, this understates the importance of London in transacting business in overseas securities.

	£bn
New York	2,700
Tokyo	2,300
London	780
NASDAQ	470
Germany	320
Paris	290

Table 1.2: Value of domestic equity market 1994
Source: London Stock Exchange Fact Book 1994

1.2.3 Trading in smaller companies

At the end of 1994 there were 937 UK companies on the Official List of The London Stock Exchange which had a market value of less than £50m. This comprised 49% of the total number of UK companies listed but, with an aggregate value of £19 bn, represented only 2.5% of the value of the whole market. This compares with 178 companies trading on the Unlisted Securities Market (USM) which had a market value of less than £50m, having a total value of £1.3 bn. There were therefore more 'small companies' on the official list than on the USM, the second tier market that is being phased out and is due to close at the end of 1996.

1.3 WHY DO COMPANIES SEEK A LISTING?

There are many reasons for the directors of a private company to obtain a trading facility in their shares. This is commonly called a listing, in London, because all companies whose shares are traded on The London Stock Exchange are eligible to have transactions in them included in the Daily Official List published by The Exchange. Such companies are said to be 'on the Official List'. The reasons for listing are not mutually exclusive, so several or all of them may influence directors and shareholders. The reasons that have been acknowledged by company directors in responses to questionnaires include:

1 *To raise new capital*: this may occur in a number of ways; through the initial public offering when the shares are first listed and through subsequent rights issues.

2 *To confer additional status*: the status conferred by being listed may enable a company to:
   (a) recruit more effectively;
   (b) obtain finance more easily and at better rates of interest;
   (c) win business.

3 *To allow shareholders to realise their investment*: the simplest and most obvious reason for a listing is to permit the trade in shares. However the ability to do this is also related to the concept of liquidity (see Chapter 2). If buyers and sellers find it difficult to find a party with whom to deal at all, or only in small quantities, or if they cannot deal at the advertised price then the shares are described as illiquid. In such circumstances the trading facility may have little advantage over a broker who matches bargains between clients.

4 *To allow shareholders to value their shares*: trading allows shareholders to value their shares for purposes such as calculating inheritance tax and pledging shares to secure a bank loan. It also satisfies shareholders' need to know what their investment is theoretically worth.

5 *To assist in growth by acquisition*: directors in potential acquisition targets may be more receptive to an approach from a listed company, with the additional status it brings. Their shareholders may also, for reasons of saving tax, want their shares to be paid for with other shares, rolling over a capital gains tax liability.

   A further point is that quoted shares are generally recognised to be worth more than if they are not quoted – this suggests that a company with a trading facility for its shares will be able to acquire other businesses more cheaply than if it does not have such a share trading facility.

6 *To reward and motivate staff*: a listing permits employees to be rewarded with share options which can be exercised and sold in the market. This may help to align the interests of employees more closely to those of the shareholders, since their reward is greater, the higher the market value of shares.

1.4 SECOND MARKETS

There are two meanings of the term 'secondary market'. On the one hand, it refers to the trading in shares after the initial flotation (which is termed the primary market). On the other hand, a secondary market is a second tier market, separate from the main stock exchange in a country, generally in the shares of smaller and younger companies. The term does not have a precise definition. We refer to these markets as second markets throughout this book, to avoid confusion.

A second market emerges because directors and shareholders of the companies want to be able to trade in the shares but they are not able or do not want to obtain a trading facility on the main stock market. They may not be able to meet the requirements of the main market or may not want to spend the money required to comply with membership, or may not want to meet the disclosure requirements. Indeed, in the UK, shares have been traded 'off-market' under the Stock Exchange's Rule 4.2 even when directors of the companies did not initiate the trading facility. A number of shareholders took it upon themselves to trade through a broker who was willing to match bargains.

Sometimes a 'customer' demand has led to the growth of completely unregulated trading through intermediaries. This sort of market is called an over-the-counter or OTC market. It has become more difficult to carry on this sort of trading in the UK since the passing of the Financial Services Act in 1986, which came into force in 1988. This Act has conferred means of protection on investors that may allow them to claim compensation from brokers or investment advisers who are deemed either to have wrongly advised them or not to have carried out their duty of care. Nonetheless, for the sophisticated investors who are thought to enter into such arrangements with their eyes open, such OTC deals are still possible.

It is such consumer pressure that has generally persuaded official exchanges to provide a formal, if cheaper and less regulated, market. The problem for the exchanges has been that the trade in the shares of smaller companies is seldom an economic proposition for themselves or their traders. However the growth of an unregulated competitor is seldom attractive to them (or to their government regulators).

1.4.1 The Unlisted Securities Market (USM)

The Unlisted Securities Market or 'USM' was established by The Stock Exchange in November 1980. It resulted from a perceived gap in the funding available to smaller, rapidly growing companies. As far back as 1931 The Macmillan Committee on Finance and Industry reported on the particular difficulties faced by companies in obtaining medium term finance in relatively small quantities. Later enquiries by The Radcliffe Committee on the Workings of the Monetary System (1959), The Bolton Committee of Enquiry on Small Firms (1971) and The Wilson Committee to Review the Functioning of Financial Institutions (1977–80) raised similar concerns. The Wilson Committee also heard evidence on the absence of a market for the shares in smaller companies that were not yet ready for the main stock exchange. The evidence put forward was to the effect that there was a weak market for new issues – companies seeking a share listing for the first time. This is illustrated in Figure 1.3 below.

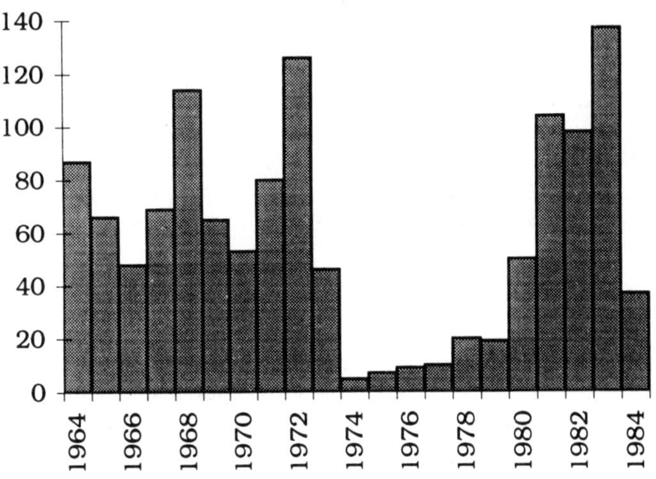

Figure 1.3: Number of new issues on the London Stock Market 1964–84

Source: London Stock Exchange Fact Books

Reasons put forward for the weak new issues market included:

- high costs of entry;
- the excessive burden of regulation.

However the very high interest rates which depressed share values in the mid-1970s were probably the major cause of this problem. It was not just the flotation of small companies that disappeared during the period but the virtual disappearance of a new issues market in companies of all sizes.

In December 1977, in response to questions raised by the Wilson Committee, The Stock Exchange issued a booklet that drew attention to the possibility of trading shares under their Rule 163(2). For many years this had allowed member firms to undertake occasional trades in unlisted securities. The brokers had to get permission for each deal that took place, which then occurred on the basis of a stockbroker matching a potential seller with a potential buyer and the trade took place outside the regulation of The Stock Exchange. The Exchange, however, reserved the right to prevent the development of continuous trading in any security which could give rise to an unregulated second market.

Following the publicity given to it, dealings under Rule 163(2) increased rapidly and the authorities at The Stock Exchange became concerned that this would indeed become an unregulated, rival market. In December 1979 they published a discussion document, 'The Stock Exchange Unlisted Securities Market', proposing a more lightly regulated market which was followed in October 1980 by full scale regulations, and on 10 November 1980 the USM was launched, with 11 companies.

The Stock Exchange Green Book set out their vision for the USM:

> 'The principal purpose is to provide a formal, regulated market designed to meet the need of those smaller, less mature companies unlikely to apply for a listing. Without such a market and some assurance of marketability for their investment, investors are liable to be less willing to take a stake.
>
> The USM will bring under the formal regulatory control of The Stock Exchange those unlisted companies whose securities were being freely traded under the provisions of Rule 163(2). That rule permits occasional bargains subject to the permission of the Council

in the shares of unlisted and private companies; it will continue to be available for that purpose but on a somewhat more restricted basis than in the recent past.'

How was the USM different from the Official List? Table 1.3 below shows, at its outset, the main points of difference.

USM	*Official List*
As little as 10% of equity in public hands	At least 25% of equity in public hands
Companies admitted on the basis of a three-year trading record, and less in certain circumstances, where funds are required to finance a 'fully researched project'	Companies admitted on a five-year trading record
No accountant's report required, a table of financial statistics to be required in its place	A formal accountant's report required
No sponsor's declaration required as to the adequacy of a new entrant's working capital	Sponsor's declaration required as to the adequacy of a new entrant's working capital
No lower capitalisation limit	Minimum capitalisation limit of £500,000

Table 1.3: Initial points of difference between the USM and Official List

Growth and decline

The USM grew rapidly throughout the 1980s, both in terms of the number of companies joining the market and the amount of money raised; this is illustrated in Figure 1.4. Between its launch in 1980 and 1989, when it began to decline, new issues on the USM only raised 4.6% of the new money raised through the Official List. However, this greatly understates the true performance and importance of the new market. Over 130 companies graduated to the Official List during that period, so the USM provided a valuable route to allow companies to obtain finance to grow. In addition, the comparison of the amounts raised through new issues on the Official List flotations was distorted by the government's privatisation programme, which brought in over £16bn.

However, despite the early success of the USM, it ended abruptly; the flow of new issues to the market declined sharply around 1989 to 1990 and has not recovered. This sudden downturn does not reflect any lack of interest from companies wanting their shares to be traded – a fact demonstrated quite clearly by the sharp rise in the number of smaller companies joining the Official List and also by growing numbers seeking permission for their shares to be traded on an occasional basis through the Stock Exchange's Rule 4.2 facility.

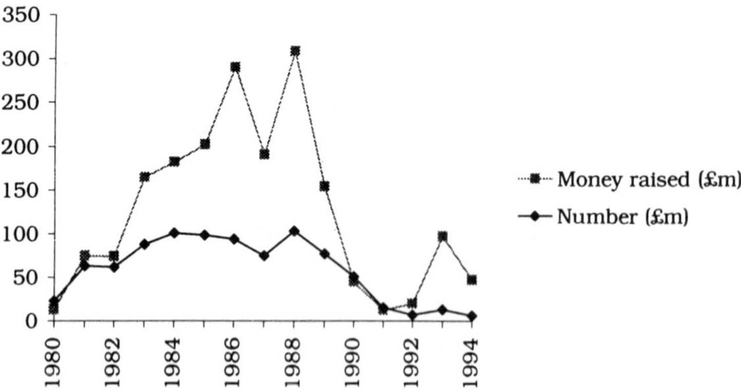

Figure 1.4: Trend of new issues on the USM – new issues and money raised
Source: London Stock Exchange

The reasons for the decline of the USM appear to have arisen partly from amendments to the rules of the Official List in 1990 to bring them into line with the requirements of the EC's Investment Services Directive. The Directive was designed to eliminate differences between European exchanges in order to increase competition and to create a single market for investment services. Some of the effects were:

1 *Greater accessibility of the Official List*: the Exchange reduced the trading record required for entry to the Official List, from five years to three: at the same time reducing that for the USM from three years to two.
2 *Converging costs*: the costs of obtaining a quotation for shares arise largely from underwriting, advertising requirements and advisers' fees. In 1990 the advertising requirements for listed companies were reduced to a similar level to those for the USM. At the same time, the practice of sponsors and advisers has led to a convergence of the work that goes into producing a USM prospectus with the listing particulars for the Official List.
3 *Intentions of the Stock Exchange*: the Exchange indicated its intention to require USM companies to have at least 25% of their shares in public hands, similar to the Official List.

The decline in image of the USM resulted in part from the 1987 crash in share prices. This should, more properly, be called a market correction since the rapid rise in both prices and share trading volumes in 1987 was unsustainable and both returned to their long-term trend of growth. The 'crash' nonetheless had a severe effect on investors' perceptions. Many investors thought of the prices at the peak as the norm rather than as an exception and were shaken by the decline. Many of the investors in smaller companies sought refuge by switching their investments to larger companies on the Official List, and USM trading volumes declined more than the Official List.

It has been argued that another factor underlying the deteriorating image of the USM was the transfer to it of small companies from The Exchange's third tier market – the Third Market – in 1990/91, with its closure. Since there had been a poor perception of the Third Market, it has been argued that some of this lack of confidence also transferred to the USM.

The shift in perceptions was important; at its peak the USM had a strong identity as a market for entrepreneurs and smaller but rapidly growing companies. A USM magazine was published, an annual dinner held, and more importantly, brokers provided extensive analysis and commentary on USM companies. In more recent years, with recession and the reduced analytical effort of major stockbrokers resulting from Big Bang in the City, trading in USM shares has declined, leading to fewer brokers following the companies, less analysis and less trading.

As Figure 1.5 illustrates, share trading of USM stocks fell proportionately further in 1988 and recovered more slowly in 1989 than trading on the Official List. The differences in performance between the two markets do not appear to have been catastrophic but, rather than seeking ways to recover the situation, the intention to close the market was announced and trading volumes on the USM fell precipitously in 1990 as confidence disappeared. While it will have taken six years for this closure actually to take place, the damage of this announcement must also have been a factor in the accelerating decline in the USM.

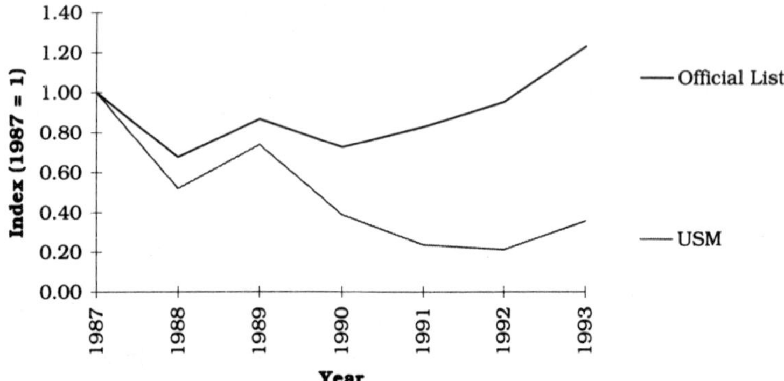

Figure 1.5: Share trading volumes on the London Stock Exchange
Source: Stock Exchange Fact Book

The Exchange is now showing a very clear commitment to AIM but in the past there has been a widely held perception among market observers that it has had little interest in or commitment to second markets. We believe that this perception, whether justified or not, has harmed the prospects for success of those second markets that the Exchange has managed. The separate management team and the considerable investment that the Exchange has put into AIM are therefore welcome and important demonstrations of confidence and commitment that will, hopefully, underpin the success of the new market.

Together with all these pressures towards convergence of the markets managed by the Exchange, amendments to the EC Listing Particulars Directive that are under consideration would allow companies to move from the USM to the Official List without having to produce listing particulars. The Exchange carried out a survey of USM companies in 1992 which confirmed that 59% intended to move to the List 'in the near future'. Of those companies which did not intend to graduate to full listing, 86% gave their reason as the cost being too high. In any case it must be realised that in early 1994 more than half (54%) of all quoted companies had a market capitalisation of less than £50m.

With the USM, therefore, acting primarily as a feeder to the List, with its differentiation having largely disappeared and with many new issues going straight to the Official List, The Exchange saw little point in retaining a separate USM and, on 1 April 1993, it announced that its merger with the Official List would take effect at the end of 1996. Companies currently on the USM will be permitted a 'free transfer' without a requirement to produce listing particulars.

1.4.2 Tertiary markets

We apply the term 'tertiary market' to the methods for trading shares in companies that are too small or have too short a track record even for the second markets. In the early 1980s a market in shares emerged that was termed the Over-The-Counter Market. This was promoted by firms such as Harvard Securities and was an unregulated market. It helped a number of companies to raise finance but also gained a reputation for being home to the fast-and-loose. It ended in 1987 as a result of the tighter regulatory regime covering brokers and the regulation introduced by the Financial Services Act.

In 1987, The Stock Exchange introduced its own tertiary market, the Third Market aimed at 'junior companies' that were too small even for the USM. It was to be an 'accessible' but nonetheless 'disciplined' market place with a suitable standard of investor protection. It provided a means for young growing companies to raise equity finance before they had established a long enough trading record to join the USM (at that time a three-year trading record was required).

Admission was open to UK companies which had already established trading or which could demonstrate the need for funds to finance a product or project which 'is fully researched and costed and where income can soon be expected to flow'[1]. There was therefore no qualifying period

[1] Booklet 'The 3rd Market', The London Stock Exchange, October 1987.

nor size requirement. As with AIM, there was no requirement for a qualifying percentage of shares to be in public hands as long as there was a reasonable prospect of an aftermarket. There were to be two market makers, though The Exchange indicated a willingness to reduce this requirement on a case-by-case basis if necessary. Order driven trading through a bulletin board facility was not available at that time. There was provision for a broker to match bargains in Third Market securities. However, AIM requires a much stronger commitment from the nominated broker to support trading.

The cost to join the market was low, with no particular requirement for a prospectus other than that laid down by the law. However, once having joined the market the continuing costs of membership, associated with shareholder circulars, were not reduced. As explained below, AIM companies have a reduced requirement to issue shareholder circulars, reducing the continuing cost of membership.

This was also a 'sponsor regulated' market as AIM is. The company had to have a sponsor and trading in its securities was suspended if it lost it. While the sponsor had responsibility for bringing the firm to market, for supervising shareholder circulars and for continuing communication with the market through the regulatory news service, it did not have the same role for providing continuing guidance to the directors as is envisaged for AIM's nominated advisers. There was also a lesser implication from the Exchange – compared with nominated advisers – that they would bear some responsibility for the conduct of their clients.

The Third Market was never a success; it attracted mostly very small companies indeed (capitalised at £1m to £2m) and there was little trading in their shares after admission. Based on the representations that have been made to the Exchange with regard to AIM, institutional investors seem to seek a higher degree of regulation at entry than the Third Market offered. Yet this higher degree of regulation is probably not appropriate to such very small companies, while slightly larger companies would join the USM. By 1991 it was decided to close the market and to assist those firms that wanted to transfer to the USM.

Does the failure of the Third Market carry warnings for AIM? We think there are some useful lessons, which do seem to have been addressed through the rules that have been announced for AIM:

1 There does not seem to be room for both an official second and a tertiary market.
2 There is a need for the Exchange to actively promote and separately manage all its markets.
3 If the first line of regulation in a market is to be a 'sponsor' or adviser then the Exchange must actively manage those sponsors in order to protect the reputation of the market. That reputation is important; it is our view that the Third Market attracted a poor reputation which tarnished the attraction of the companies whose shares traded through it.
4 'Visibility' of securities traded and support for their trading are important issues.

There does seem to be a continuing demand from some investors and companies for a form of inexpensive and lightly regulated share dealing on an over-the-counter basis. This has manifested itself twice in the UK in recent years, as illustrated above, and at least one of the market makers in smaller companies seems prepared to 'make a market' off-Exchange after the ending of the Rule 4.2 trading facility. This small scale requirement, with investor protection limited to that demanded by the Financial Services Act 1986 and the rules of the organisations that regulate investment business in the UK, does not suit a regulated market. As discussed later, the development of this off-market trading may be greatly promoted if brokers can publish their prices and information about companies through the Internet. This would allow many private as well as institutional investors to have access to security prices and possibly to be aware of buy and sell orders easily and inexpensively. Information on companies trading on NASDAQ is already published in this way. It is not clear whether such information would constitute an investment advertisement and be regulated under the Financial Services Act. In the meantime, before such facilities are widely used, off-market trading does not provide a real alternative to AIM because:

1 Vetting of companies for suitability (eg do they have the financial controls one would expect from a publicly traded company?) will be minimal.
2 Shares traded off-market are generally less easily traded than those on AIM (there is less likely to be a firm, continuous price quoted and widely advertised for two-way trades).

The reinvented USM

At the same time as announcing the closure of the USM, a working party was announced to look into the merits of a new second market: a reinvented USM. This apparent contradiction probably resulted from two pressures. On the one hand, the venture capital institutions and other City investors seem to have been keen for a second market and lobbied the Exchange in an effort to persuade it to institute one. However, another reason for the Exchange sponsoring a second market may have been the refusal of second markets to go away. As the factors outlined above caused the USM to die away, trading in companies' shares under Rule 4.2 grew. While statistics have not been kept by the Stock Exchange for earlier years, it recorded trades in 264 companies worth £482.4m during the year to 30 June 1994. Further, new issues on this unregulated market raised over £112m from investors during 1994.

The Stock Exchange cannot feel comfortable with the emergence of new markets, however small, that may eventually become serious competitors. NASDAQ in the USA began as a second market and was characterised in its early days as embodying the 'wild west'. However by 1994 it had achieved a size equal to 70% of the market capitalisation of its main rival, the New York Stock Exchange (NYSE). It had companies such as Microsoft, Apple Corporation and Reuters listing on it rather than on the NYSE.

In addition, the Exchange felt uncomfortable that it had responsibility without power; investors looked to it for protection although it had no formal regulatory obligation nor any jurisdiction over the 4.2 Market. Nonetheless it did have quite a deep involvement as shown in **1.4.3** below. Under the Exchange's new rule book, published in 1994, member firms no longer need permission to deal in shares 'off-Exchange'. The rule itself is therefore an anomaly, since members do not need it in order to deal. However, many member firms prefer to trade under the umbrella of the Exchange, partly to avoid association with what might be viewed as a slightly disreputable, unregulated market.

But what sort of second market would be appropriate? The terms of reference for the working party on the new market said:

> 'There was a perception among some of the respondents to the USM consultative document that following the demise of the USM it will be more difficult for small companies to raise capital through a public flotation. Also the regulatory regime and costs of both the full List and USM are regarded by some as being too onerous to be attractive to a number of companies which are suffering from a lack of financing opportunities from other sources.'

Draft rules for AIM were published in the late summer of 1994 and seemed to describe a market closer to trading under Rule 4.2 than the USM. However, the Exchange received a very strong response during its consultation period, with over 130 separate submissions. There was, in particular, a powerful body of opinion pressing for compulsory sponsorship of companies seeking to issue shares on AIM. The widespread feeling was that without this the market would attract unsuitable companies and would lose credibility. At the same time, a number of UK based venture capital institutions which were expressing these views were also working with bodies such as the Paris Bourse, NASDAQ and the European Venture Capital Association to promote a European wide second market in the form of the proposed EASDAQ, which would compete with AIM. This market is intended to have a high level of supervision similar to that for Official Listing.

The rules for AIM were published in early 1995 and many observers have been very impressed by the responsiveness of the Exchange to the criticism of its initial proposals for the new market. The final rules have striven to retain features that should permit the cost of flotation and continued membership to be significantly lower than for Official Listing, while strengthening the regulatory and supervisory regime compared with the original proposals.

1.4.3 Rule 4.2 trading

This facility for member firms to trade in shares 'off-Exchange', on a matched bargain basis, has been available for a long time, originally as Rule 163.2, then 535.2 and, under the latest version of the Stock Exchange's rule book, Rule 4.2. In 1978, in response to representations for a second market, the Exchange drew attention to the ability to seek permission to trade on an occasional basis. The permission was then extended to cover all trades over a 12-month period, which was usually automatically renewed every 12 months. In the late 1980s the Exchange further extended the trading under this rule to allow member firms to quote bid and offer prices as well as matching bargains, resulting in a continuous market. To add to the appearance of a market rather than a mere trading facility, the Exchange checked and recorded trades and published prices of bargains in the Daily Official List, settled some of them through its Talisman system and co-operated on a 'Non-SEAQ Noticeboard' where brokers could post orders. There was therefore a curious situation of a market existing under the umbrella of the Exchange, yet without its regulation.

The rule itself states:

> 4.2 (a) A member firm may apply to the Exchange for permission to effect transactions on the Domestic Equity Market in securities other than fixed interest securities of a company which is incorporated in the United Kingdom or the Republic of Ireland which are not listed or admitted to trading on the USM, or if so listed or admitted, are for the time being suspended or prohibited to be dealt on the Exchange.
>
> (b) Applications other than those in relation to securities which are suspended or prohibited to be dealt on the Exchange shall be accompanied by:
> (i) the latest set of audited accounts of the company; and
> (ii) any prospectus or circular produced since the latest balance sheet date.
>
> (c) A permission under paragraph (a):
> (i) in relation to securities other than those which are suspended or prohibited runs for a period of twelve months from the date of the last transaction;
> (ii) in relation to securities which are suspended or prohibited to be dealt on the Exchange, must be obtained in respect of each proposed transaction.

An article in the Stock Exchange Quarterly tells us: 'the Exchange checks these documents [accounts, prospectuses and circulars] to ensure that the company has a genuine business and that the report and accounts are not qualified.'

Companies recording trades under this rule have increased steadily from 216 in 1990 to some 340 by mid-1995 (see Table 1.4). Their average market capitalisation is between £5m and £10m. Nonetheless, five companies moved from this trading facility to the Official List in 1993, four with market capitalisation in excess of £50m.

	1990	1991	1992	1993	1994
New applications	68	90	73	79	127
No. of companies traded (year-end approx)	216	220	220	240	340

Table 1.4: Companies recording trades under Rule 4.2
Source: Stock Exchange Quarterly

What sort of companies have their securities traded through Rule 4.2? They fall into two main categories as follows:

1 Established companies seeking a means for investors to sell if they want. They may be debt or other securities of companies which have ordinary shares on the USM or the Official List. Some of these companies have been on the Official List or USM and have been unable to continue to meet the requirements or are unwilling to sustain the cost. In practice this facility is generally of use for small parcels of shares since there is insufficient liquidity for large trades except on a matched bargain basis. A few companies even have shares traded on 4.2 without their active consent, where shareholders initiated the trading facility.
2 Growing companies seeking to issue new shares to finance expansion.

With the establishment of AIM, the Stock Exchange has indicated that it will end continuous trading under Rule 4.2, although there will be a period of grace until 29 September 1995. The Exchange has stated that by that time companies whose shares are traded under the rule will have to decide between – applying to join the Official List, joining AIM or trading off-market. As discussed in Chapter 14, there are other choices. These include joining NASDAQ (an American exchange) or other foreign second markets. Rule 4.2 will be rewritten to permit only trading in securities that have been suspended from the Official List. The intention is to allow infrequent trades of Officially Listed companies, if they are a special case, which is a reversion towards the original purpose of the first incarnation of this Rule as 163.2.

The reinvented 4.2 market

Our research shows that there are a number of companies, whose shares traded under Rule 4.2, that do not want to join AIM and were quite happy with the way things were. Some very big companies are traded on 4.2, such as Weetabix (market capitalisation around £200m) and National Car Parks (whose market capitalisation is in excess of £600m). As referred to previously, there are even companies whose shareholders have independently initiated trading rather than the directors of the company. There seems to be every indication that a number of these companies will continue to be traded completely outside the jurisdiction of the Exchange. There also seems to be no reason why there should not be new entrants to this informal market. For example, companies formed to take advantage of the tax reliefs provided under the Enterprise Investment Scheme may perceive very little demand from investors for trading facilities. Their investors would lose their tax relief if they sell within five years. However, there may be a few investors who need cash in the short term and are willing to sacrifice their tax relief. For them, trading on a matched bargain basis through a broker may be a convenient solution. Trading off-market is discussed in more detail in Chapter 14.

CHAPTER 2

How shares trade

2.1 GENERAL BACKGROUND

This chapter provides a general background to share trading on the London Stock Exchange and covers a number of the points of difference that apply to AIM. Further detailed information is also given in para **7.8** which describes the regulations applying to market making on AIM.

Shares traded on the Official List are primarily traded on a screen based system called SEAQ and transactions are mainly settled through the Talisman system of the Stock Exchange. However, there is nothing to stop two shareholders agreeing to deal between themselves without going through the Exchange at all. Indeed, the Tradepoint system, described later, is designed to work as a computerised trading system between shareholders. However, member firms of the Exchange (brokers) must trade AIM securities with each other through the Exchange.

The London Stock Exchange operates through a mechanism called market making, sometimes called a quotation driven system. One or more member firms of the Exchange will make a market in a particular security through offering to buy at a price called the bid price, or to sell at an offer price. They will publicise, through the computer system of the Stock Exchange, these two prices together with the number of shares for which this price is guaranteed. Thus, if the price quoted by a market maker for ordinary shares in Company A is 20 to 22p for 10,000 shares then anyone can ring up and do a deal, up to this number of shares at that price. They do not have to specify whether they are buyers or sellers in order to get a firm price. If the screen system only gives prices for 10,000 shares and someone wants a price for 20,000 shares then they must ring and ask for one. This price may not be the same as the displayed price.

Less liquid securities which only have one market maker can be traded on the Stock Exchange Alternative Trading Service (SEATS). This provides for a mixture of market making and order driven trading because not all securities will have a market maker. Under order driven trading, someone who wants to buy shares in Company A, say for 18 pence, will input this, through a member firm, into the system where it will be displayed, awaiting a seller at this price.

An enhanced version, called SEATS PLUS, has been introduced from 12 June 1995, coinciding with the start of trading on AIM. With SEATS PLUS going live a week before the new market commenced, it was hoped that any teething problems with the system would be resolved before trading commenced. AIM shares are to be traded on a segment of SEATS PLUS which:

- allows more than one market maker's quote to be displayed;
- can show indicative and mid-market prices rather than a firm quote unless another market maker is displaying firm quotes.

A mid-market price is the mid-point between the bid and offer prices. It gives little indication of what these are unless the spread, ie the difference between them, is quoted.

A market maker is obliged to quote firm two-way prices when someone enquires by telephone during what is known as the 'mandatory quote period' of the Exchange. For dealings after hours they are not obliged to do so.

SEATS PLUS will allow member firms to use the screen based system to execute orders that are held on the 'central order book' maintained by the Stock Exchange.

2.2 SEATS

The Stock Exchange Alternative Trading Service was launched in November 1992 to provide 'an efficient trading platform for less liquid shares' which have fewer than two market makers (ie one or none). The main market system, SEAQ, is specifically a mechanism to deal with competing market makers' quotes. If a company has only one market maker it is automatically transferred to SEATS.

SEATS provides a central display for customer orders in parallel with displaying the quotations of a single market maker. It is a continuation of the experimentation that had led to the Company Bulletin Board (April 1992) which was also designed to find a less costly way of making smaller, less frequent trades in smaller companies. With less trading occurring in such shares there is less willingness for anyone to act as market maker, tying up capital, and fewer buyers or sellers available to make trades. The market makers were concerned that the rules requiring the announcement of trades meant that they might have an obligation to buy or sell shares in a market where there were few buyers or sellers available and their need had been advertised. The market price might easily move against them in such circumstances, giving them a substantial exposure. Such intermittent trading can also give rise to large fluctuations in price as a result of a single transaction.

The Company Bulletin Board had displayed orders for less liquid shares and enabled trading without the need for a market maker. While it offered a low cost method of trading less liquid shares, there was no evidence that it had affected levels of turnover in them. In some cases, Bulletin Board stocks lacked the facility for an immediate trade to take place, which is provided by a market maker who is willing to 'take a position'. In other cases, brokers emerged who were effectively acting as market makers in particular stocks. As a result, SEATS saw the merger of the Bulletin Board with the concept of a single market maker for each share, though the Bulletin Board aspect of SEATS remains as an alternative for companies without a market maker.

Where there is no market maker registered in a security, the corporate broker to the company takes on the responsibility of using their best endeavours to match buyers with sellers. They are also responsible for supplying information about the company to the SEATS Controller at the Exchange who then puts it into the computer system. Market makers are attracted to companies where there is a sufficient trade in the shares for them to make a profit from trading. Factors that contribute to weak trading include too few shares in the hands of the public and poor 'visibility' of the company, through insufficient publicity about it. As a result of having no market maker, a company may experience difficulty in raising further equity funding from investors, who may be concerned about their ability to trade their shares.

As at the end of 1994, there were 106 companies whose shares traded on SEATS and trading in their shares was over £420m during the year.

2.2.1 The TOPIC page

Information on SEATS stocks is displayed on a TOPIC computer page that is supplied to subscribers through a number of possible resellers of the electronic information supplied by the Exchange.

The page shows the following background information:

- date of last update of the information;
- SEDOL Code (a unique code given to each company admitted by the Exchange);
- industry sector;
- approximate percentage of the shares available to be traded on the market;
- expected date for announcement of final and interim results;
- final or interim profit/(loss) after tax;
- final or interim turnover;
- net interim dividend or both net interim and final dividend;
- volume of shares traded during the previous complete 12-month period;
- volume of shares traded during the current month.

This information must be supplied by the broker within 24 hours of the announcement of the company's interim and final results.

The page also shows the last ten trades though these are limited to market maker non-risk and broker dealer trades. The information displayed includes the date of the transaction, the two brokers involved, the price and quantity of shares. The idea is that business transacted with investors is publicised to show other actual or potential investors a picture of the frequency, price and size of trades. Where the market maker has taken a position for the purposes of their own dealing book this does not have to be displayed except at the end of the day, when such positions are shown in aggregate.

2.2.2 Market makers

The market maker must display a continuous two-way price during the mandatory quote period from 8.30 am to 4.30 pm. However, this displayed price may, in certain circumstances, be indicative rather than a firm commitment to deal at that price (see **7.8** for further details). They are obliged to deal at their displayed firm prices at up to their displayed sizes. The minimum order size at which the market maker may quote is 500 shares (see **7.8** for further details).

There are over 30 market makers on SEAQ, over 50 on SEAQ International, and 3 on SEATS. AIM is likely to start with 2 or 3 although a number of brokers may register in respect of securities they have brought to market.

2.2.3 The order board

Associated with the TOPIC page for each security traded on the market there is an order page displaying outstanding orders together with the broker, whether it is buy or sell, the quantity and the price. When there is a market maker quoting a firm price in the security, the order board must also show a firm price. When there is only an indicative price or no market maker, then the orders may show only an indicative price – to be confirmed if another party wishes to deal. This indication must represent a genuine desire to trade at or about that price and a broker may be disciplined if they will not do so. All firm orders automatically become indicative when there is a company announcement. This gives the brokers a chance to remove or amend them: after 30 minutes they revert to being firm. Prices for orders may also become indicative if the computer systems of the Exchange or market makers cannot cope with the volume of trading or if they break down. They are always indicative outside the mandatory quote period.

When a broker wants to use the order board facility they must telephone through their buy or sell orders as well as their cancellations or amendments of orders to the SEATS Controller who inputs them into the system.

Before a market maker executes any business in a SEATS security they must first check whether there are any firm orders at the same or a better price than they intend to deal at. If there is such an order then the market maker must satisfy that order as far as possible (given the number of shares the market maker offers a firm price in).

Similarly, before the market maker changes the price of their quote they must check the order board and settle any orders at an equal or more competitive price.

If there is a market maker in a security then a broker must report the price of any proposed trade to them. The market maker then has the right to fulfil the trade under certain circumstances.

2.2.4 Announcements

The main TOPIC page for a security shows an A in blue at the top right-hand corner of the screen. This alerts the viewer to go to the pages displaying the Regulatory News Service to get the text of the announcement.

Similarly, the screen shows an X in blue at the top right-hand corner to show when the securities are trading ex-dividend or ex-rights etc.

It is incumbent on a company whose securities are traded on AIM to ensure that all its announcements satisfy four conditions – that they are:

- sufficient;
- accurate;
- not misleading;
- timely.

The announcements should be sufficient to give all investors the information they need to make an informed assessment of a situation. This is the overriding requirement of the Exchange which is clarified by the further conditions which are imposed. It is just as important that announcements do not omit information that would enable an investor to make an informed judgement. It is never acceptable to make an inaccurate announcement, whether intentionally or inadvertently, since that may give rise to a false market in the securities. Any inaccuracy must be corrected as soon as it comes to light. Finally, even an accurate announcement may mislead investors through its phrasing, and great care must be taken to avoid this.

Information is not sufficient for the investor to make an informed decision if it is not available at the appropriate time. News should, therefore, be announced 'without delay' to the market as a whole. If it is withheld until some investors find out about it from other sources, that gives them an unfair trading advantage. The Exchange insists that great care must be taken to avoid this situation.

It is not possible to define the term 'without delay' because circumstances will differ. However, the principle is that an announcement should be made immediately the circumstances giving rise to it become apparent and there needs to be a good reason for any deviation from this.

Market expectations

One of the most common reasons for making an announcement is when it becomes clear to company management that trading performance is not going to match market expectations. This applies when results are likely to exceed as well as when they fall short. In practice there are very few occasions when a company announces that the market has underestimated the likely outcome for the year. Such expectations may be gauged from the forecasts of stockbrokers' analysts, newspaper, newsletter and magazine reports. The company's broker will usually indicate what institutional investors expect from their regular contacts. The strongest and most reliable indicator of expectations is likely to be the price of the issuer's securities. If the issuer becomes aware that their own expectations are going to be significantly incorrect then it is likely that the market too is going to have incorrect expectations.

If these misapprehensions appear to be widely held and if they are material then an announcement must be made. Something is generally held to be material if it relates to more than 10% inaccuracy in profit forecasts and there would seldom be any doubt if the disparity was as high as 20% that an announcement would be required. The need for an announcement is often a matter of judgement, particularly when it is not clear quite what the consensus of the market is. A company whose financial results are normally volatile might need a higher threshhold for making an announcement than one whose trading history showed a steady progression.

Exemption

A company can seek dispensation from the Exchange if it is felt that an announcement may 'prejudice its legitimate interests'. This might apply, for example, to negotiations with banks for refinancing or with a potential business partner for a deal that may transform the prospects of the company. The Exchange has to balance the needs of the company with preserving an orderly market and protecting investors. It must therefore consider the interests of investors, for example, who may buy or sell shares that are likely to move dramatically in price a short while afterwards.

Avoidance of selective release of information

One of the guiding principles of the Exchange is that the whole market should have access to the same information. However, this apparently simple requirement demands significant interpretation and judgement. Company directors will meet substantial investors, brokers' analysts, writers for newspapers and newsletters – what can they reveal and what would give unfair advantage to a small interest group?

The Exchange makes it clear that companies should not disclose 'significant data' and adds that financial information clearly falls into this category. It would therefore be improper to answer an analyst's questions about company expectations of divisional sales or profits. Yet it is probably acceptable to give 'deep background' information about trading philosophy, management structure, market trends – as long as these would not enable the recipient to make a forecast that would differ significantly from the current market expectations.

It is often hard to balance this directive against the need to manage market expectations to some degree. A director acting as spokesman for the company is often confronted by a stockbroker's analyst presenting a detailed profit & loss account and cash flow forecast by division and seeking some guidance as to whether it is reasonable. While the widespread practice has been to go some way, at least, towards steering the analysts in the right direction this would appear to be contrary to the wishes of the Exchange.

2.3 TRADING

Trading on SEATS is conducted over the telephone. Once agreed, the SEATS Controller must be notified within three minutes so that the order can be removed from the system.

2.3.1 Monitoring of trading

AIM securities will be subject to the Exchange's Market Supervision and Surveillance Departments in the same way as the Official List and the USM.

The Supervision Department monitors the markets to try to detect possible fraud, price manipulation, insider dealing etc. Significant price rises occurring prior to announcements, for instance, attract its attention. In such circumstances it can carry out investigations.

The Market Surveillance Department supervises trading. It monitors market makers' quotes as well as ensuring that trades are properly reported within the time specified by the Exchange.

2.3.2 Reporting and settlement

The rules for reporting and settling trades are the same for AIM as they are for the Official List.

All trades, including the price and quantity of shares, are published the following day in the Exchange's Daily Official List together with market maker quotes at the end of business.

AIM securities may be settled through Talisman, the system operated by the Stock Exchange, or by any other method they choose. They may, for instance, choose to have all trades settled through their registrars or specialist settlements houses. While this may be cumbersome, it may be cheaper in cases where there are few trades in the shares.

The rules applying to AIM require that transfers of shares are registered within 14 days of receipt of the transfer documentation. However, the Exchange has produced a Code of Good Practice which recommends one or two business days.

Until 1994 the Exchange worked on two-week periods called accounts. Any trades during this account were due for settlement on the last day, with special rules applying to trades at the end of the period. This has now been changed to a rolling settlement system, where trades are due to be settled ten days after they are made. For the Official List but not for AIM, the target becomes a five-day settlement from June 1995.

The account system made it possible for someone to sell securities that they did not have, in the hope that the price would fall and they could then be bought for a cheaper price in the market. This practice is called selling short. Rolling settlement does not prevent short selling but the shorter periods over which it can be done without needing to roll-over the transaction reduces its attractions.

The mirror image to short selling is buying a stock heavily in the hope of driving up its price and then selling within the account, so that the two settlements due on the same day will match each other, leaving a profit. This practice is called buying long.

There are two slightly different reporting and settlement procedures: private client and institutional settlement. In both cases each side of the trade is reported by the broker or brokers involved to the Stock Exchange's checking service. When the two sides of the bargain are matched they are sent to be entered on the Stock Exchange's computerised Talisman system.

Whoever is selling shares must deliver the share certificate and a signed share transfer form (called a Talisman Sold Transfer form) to their broker who lodges them at the Exchange with the Talisman office. They are then sent on to the registrar of the company whose shares are being sold who transfers them into the name of SEPON Ltd. This is a nominee company for the Stock Exchange.

On settlement day, Talisman credits the stock to the account of the market maker to whom the broker acting for the seller sold them. The market maker pays for the stock via the Exchange to the seller's broker who, in turn, makes payment to the seller. The stock is held within the SEPON account, for the market maker who bought it.

If the market maker also sold some or all of the stock then, on settlement day, the Talisman system debits the market maker's SEPON account with the amount of stock bought by the client. The Talisman system also prints a transfer form called a Talisman Bought Transfer (TBT). This is sent to the registrar of the company whose shares have been dealt in, who transfers the stock from SEPON Ltd into the name of the buyer. In a mirror image of the sale transaction, payment is made by the buyer to the broker who passes it to the market maker, through the Exchange.

Any company whose shares are actively traded will have a large number of shares registered in the name SEPON at any time. They may be held as 'trading stock' by one or more market makers or they may be in the process of moving between sellers and buyers.

The difference between an institution and a private client in this process is that the institution is able to deliver share certificates directly to the Exchange and can make or receive payment as one net amount on all transactions being settled on a particular day. This is done through the Exchange's Institutional Net Settlement (INS) service.

There is a project to automate settlement through a computer driven, paperless system, which is sponsored by the Bank of England. It replaces a previous project sponsored by the Exchange called Taurus, which was cancelled in 1993. The new project is called CREST and is planned to come into operation in 1996. This is intended to be an optional system that will prove acceptable to the majority of investors and trades going through the market. It will work side-by-side with systems that will still issue paper share certificates. When it is introduced the CREST system will be applicable to AIM as well as Official List securities.

2.3.3 Information about companies

While smaller companies whose shares are traded on AIM are unlikely to receive significant coverage in the newspapers compared with larger companies on the Official List, there are a number of sources for investors seeking information. These include: *The Investors Chronicle*, which covers smaller as well as larger companies; *Small Company Investor*, a bimonthly magazine covering smaller companies; occasional news items in daily newspapers; enquiries through a stockbroker, who will have access to information through announcements made on the Exchange's Regulatory News Service (RNS).

For companies interested in communicating with investors there is a company news service called Newstrack, which is owned by J P Jenkins, one of the leading market makers in smaller company securities. It is available through the major news vendors: Reuters, Bloomberg, QST and ICV, meaning that virtually all dealing rooms and the press will have access to it. These services are also available internationally. Newstrack proposes to make information available on the Internet, giving private investors easy access to it. Companies subscribe (currently £2,000 per annum) to have information about them posted on the screens. This includes financial information, company activities and press releases as well as share prices. The RNS is limited to price sensitive information that must be announced under the rules of the Exchange, while Newstrack will post summaries of all press releases. However, in practice, most matters that a company might want to announce for public relations purposes might be said to have a price sensitive potential.

Once the market is established, with a substantial number of securities available to be traded, then an index of AIM securities may be initiated. There are no plans to do so at present.

2.3.4 Liquidity

Liquidity is a description of the ease of trading in shares. There is no universally agreed definition of the term albeit that people generally know what they mean by it. There are three different effects of shares in a company being illiquid:

1 *Speed of dealing*: placing an order on SEATS may take some time to find a matching buyer or seller.
2 *Volume of dealing*: it may prove difficult or impossible to find someone to deal at all in a large number of shares.

3 *Price*: a quoted price may be indicative and an actual transaction may only occur at an unattractive price. As part of the same issue, a market maker may quote a very wide spread between the bid and offer price.

Lack of liquidity is caused by there being insufficient shares 'in the market'. This may arise from:

1 The company being small and having few shares.
2 The board or controlling shareholders having too high a proportion of the shares and allowing too few in 'free float'.
3 Too few shares in the hands of people who are willing to trade, which may be due to a high proportion of its shares being in the hands of individuals or institutions holding for the long term.

Conversely, liquidity is enhanced by having a high proportion of the shares widely spread, brokers or journalists providing analysis of the company and an active market maker or broker promoting trading. Each company on AIM will reach its own agreements with nominated advisers and Brokers as to work they will perform and fees they will charge. Most observers are agreed that liquidity for companies traded on AIM will be helped if those agreements include a requirement for them to produce regular brokers' reports to inform shareholders of developments and trends and to stimulate the market.

Liquidity is also something that changes over time. It is affected both by news relating to a particular security and to the market as a whole. If there is a profit warning or some other shock relating to a company's prospects then it is likely that market makers will reduce the number of shares for which they are willing to offer a firm price and will widen the spread between bid and offer price. This makes the securities less liquid. It may be more of an issue for the smaller companies which are likely to trade on AIM and which are likely to have less information, news and analysis in the public domain. This is probably a result of the size of the company rather than the market on which it trades. With fewer followers there are fewer potential investors willing to bet on recovery.

The wider economy also affects liquidity. Experience has shown that trading has fallen most in the shares of smaller companies during recession as there has been a 'flight to quality', with smaller companies finding comparatively less trading in their shares. Trading on the USM fell comparatively more than on the Official List following the Crash of 1987 and we would expect the same effect to apply to AIM in future recessions or shocks to the trading system. The message is that in times of such stress, as described above, smaller company shares become comparatively harder to trade than larger company shares, whether the share trades on AIM or the Official List.

CHAPTER 3

Regulation of securities markets in the UK

3.1 THE SECURITIES AND INVESTMENTS BOARD (SIB)

The framework for regulation of securities markets in the UK was set in place by the Financial Services Act 1986 and it was subsequently added to and amended by regulation through statutory instruments. The Act came into force on 28 April 1988. The Securities and Investments Board (SIB) was set up as a government agency under the control of the Treasury to oversee investment business in the UK. It oversees the following:

1 *Recognised Investment Exchanges*: these include the London Stock Exchange, London International Financial Futures and Options Exchange (LIFFE), London Commodities Exchange and others. These exchanges establish, monitor compliance with and enforce rules for members carrying out investment business. They are granted exemption from needing authorisation to carry on investment business, which therefore allows them to operate.
2 *Self Regulating Organisations*: individuals and organisations carrying on investment business are able to set up self regulating organisations to regulate them. These are financed through their own subscriptions. The three established to date are the Securities and Futures Authority (SFA – dealers and advisers on securities and derivatives), Investment Management Regulatory Organisation (IMRO – fund managers) and the Personal Investment Authority (PIA – life assurance and unit trust salesmen and financial intermediaries).

These bodies must institute procedures to protect the public from incompetence and fraud.

3 *Recognised Professional Bodies*: including the professional organisations of actuaries, accountants, solicitors and insurance brokers these professional bodies establish appropriate rules and procedures to cover investment business carried out by their members.

A stockbroking firm will therefore be a member of the London Stock Exchange and must observe its rules. They will also be a member of the SFA, which will regulate its activities in a professional sense.

3.1.1 The London Stock Exchange

The London Stock Exchange has an additional role since it was appointed a 'Competent Authority' under the Financial Services Act to supervise companies which issue their securities on the Exchange. It has formulated and enforces Listing Rules to regulate not only admission to trading but also continuing obligations of companies and their directors.

3.1.2 The City Code on takeovers and mergers

Another aspect of regulation is the City Code on Takeovers and Mergers which provides a framework of rules to cover the conduct of all parties in such transactions. It is overseen by the Panel on Takeovers and Mergers, whose membership is partly appointed by the Bank of England and partly made up of representatives of various organisations such as the Confederation of British Industry and the Stock Exchange. The Code does not have the weight of law but, in practice, anyone deliberately refusing to observe it would be denied access to the UK capital markets. They would probably be officially or unofficially excluded by the Securities and Investments Board, by the self regulating organisations and the Stock Exchange. Therefore a company and its directors that deliberately flouted the Code would find themselves unable to obtain professional assistance from members of the Stock Exchange, merchant banks, clearing banks and possibly even from accountants and solicitors.

PART TWO

Guide to the Regulations

CHAPTER 4

Admitting a security to AIM

The following commentary (throughout Part Two) is based closely on the Changes to the Rules of the London Stock Exchange, published on 15 February 1995. It also draws from legislation and other relevant sources. References given in brackets are either to relevant chapters and paragraphs of the Rules of the London Stock Exchange or to paragraphs of the Public Offer of Securities Regulations 1995 (POS Regulations). References to the AIM Rules are to Chapters 16 and 17 of the Stock Exchange Rules.

4.1 ELIGIBILITY

The rules do not lay down any qualifying restrictions on market capitalisation, length of trading record, continuity of management or the percentage or type of shares that are to be in the hands of the public.

The only constraints on a company that wishes its securities to be traded on AIM are practical ones. The overriding practical considerations are the ability of shareholders to trade their securities in the aftermarket and the ability of the issuer to interest investors successfully in subscribing for new securities in the first place.

1 *Ability to trade*: securing a trading facility on AIM may give prestige to a firm. However, the main reason for seeking such a facility must be to give investors the opportunity to trade their securities. Will there be continuous trading, permitting potential buyers or sellers to

deal for the number of shares they want at or near a price quoted for the security? For example, if a company is very small and is only releasing a small proportion of its shares to be traded on AIM then there will only be a small number of shares with a low total value to be traded. With small and infrequent trades it is unlikely that there will be a market maker interested in taking positions. In such circumstances are there other practical reasons for trading on AIM?

2 *Ability to raise finance*: many companies will seek to raise equity finance through AIM. To achieve this they will need to offer securities that are attractive to investors. One of those attractions will be an ability to trade in the securities, another will be a convincing case that the securities will provide an attractive return commensurate with the perceived level of risk.

The issuer of securities to be traded on AIM must be an incorporated body and those securities must be freely transferable.

1 *Incorporation*: this means that the issuer must be a company, if it is established in the UK, or it must be some similar type of legal entity established in another country (Rule 16.1.a).

2 *Freely transferable securities*: the company must be legally permitted to issue freely transferable securities. If it is established in the UK the company must be a 'Public Limited Company' and its Articles of Association must permit the free transfer of shares. This requirement is subject to an exemption under s 212 of the UK Companies Act 1985 which provides for companies to be able to demand disclosure of the beneficial ownership of shares. There have been many instances of hostile bidders building up shareholdings in different nominee names to avoid detection of their stake building and s 212 gives companies some defence against this secrecy. If the registered holder does not give the information required within a reasonable time then the issuer is permitted to prevent transfer of the shares and suspend their voting rights (CA 1985 s 212). While there is no provision in the AIM Rules for any similar legislation overseas to be given the same status, in practice it would be respected.

4.1.1 The discretion of the Stock Exchange

The Stock Exchange reserves the right to make the admission of securities to AIM subject to any special condition it thinks is appropriate. While this is to be 'in the interests of protecting investors' it gives them wide discretion and permits them to deal with circumstances not foreseen at the time the Rules were published. The Exchange cannot currently foresee refusing admission to a company conforming to the basic requirements.

It may prove important that just as there is no minimum size that must be attained for a company to join AIM, there is no maximum either. An issuer can retain the tax reliefs available to investors and remain on AIM whatever size it may grow to. One caveat to this is that if very large companies are traded on AIM then the Treasury may feel that the market is no longer different from the Official List and that it should not have distinct tax advantages. It is likely therefore that there will emerge informal pressures for large companies to move to the Official List in due course.

4.2 THE SECURITIES

Securities traded on AIM can be of any type, whether ordinary shares, preference shares, warrants, convertibles, debt securities or something else. However, most securities that are traded are likely to be ordinary shares and it is clearly important to issue a security that will find investors. For this reason non-voting shares and more exotic securities may find less favour than ordinary shares. However, warrants offering investors the right to subscribe in the future at a predetermined price, have been popular on the 4.2 Market.

Family companies often wish to raise capital for growth but are reluctant to cede voting control. This cannot be achieved through provisions in the Articles disallowing single ownership of large blocs of shares nor can voting be restricted in such circumstances. All securities traded on AIM must be freely transferable and there can be no disincentives to transferability. This does not prevent companies from issuing securities with restricted voting rights. This can be done on the Official List too, but has proved unpopular with investors.

The securities must all be traded on AIM (Rule 16.1.c). For example, there must not be a situation where only some ordinary shares could be traded on AIM.

4.3 CONTINUING DUTIES OF THE ISSUER OF SECURITIES

The issuer of securities has continuing duties which are additional to those of a public company whose securities are not traded on a stock exchange. These are detailed below.

4.3.1 Adviser and broker

The issuer must appoint and continue to have at all times:

- a nominated adviser; and
- a nominated broker

which may be the same firm (see **7.3** and **7.4** for details of their duties). The resignation or dismissal of the nominated adviser followed by a failure to replace them within a month will lead to cancellation of the trading facility (see **7.1**).

4.3.2 Publish an interim report

The issuer must publish an interim report as well as annual accounts, although the interim accounts need not be audited (Rule 16.19.f). The interim report must be published within four months of the end of the financial period. Its content is not defined in the AIM regulations but it would seem reasonable to follow the requirements set out in the Listing Rules for the Official List (paras 12.46 to 12.59), which are:

1 Report on activities and the profit or loss during the period. Such report should:
   (a) enable investors to make an informed assessment of trends in the issuer's business;
   (b) indicate any special factors that have affected trading during the period;
   (c) refer to the group's prospects (this is qualified in two respects; the reference should be 'as far as possible' and it should only be in respect of the current financial year).

2 The figures given in any report should show:
   (a) net turnover;
   (b) profit/(loss) before taxation and extraordinary items;
   (c) taxation on profits (UK, share of associated undertakings and overseas taxation to be shown separately if material);
   (d) minority interests;
   (e) profit or loss attributable to shareholders before extraordinary items;
   (f) extraordinary items (net of taxation);
   (g) profit or loss attributable to shareholders;
   (h) dividends paid and proposed;
   (i) earnings per share;
   (j) comparative figures for the corresponding period of the previous financial year.

While there is no statutory requirement for an interim balance sheet nor anything contained in the Listing Rules, many companies on the Official List now publish one because of pressure from investors and a recognition that it represents best practice.

As with other documents circulated to shareholders, six copies of the interim report should be sent to the Company Announcements Office.

4.3.3 Annual accounts

The issuer must publish annual accounts which conform to certain requirements that are additional to company law. They should:

1 Be prepared in accordance with UK Accounting Standards or US Accounting Standards or International Accounting Standards as well as with the national law in the country in which the issuer is established.
2 Be published within six months of the end of the financial period.
3 Include the name and address of the nominated adviser and, if different, the nominated broker.

4.3.4 Registration of share transfers

The issuer must ensure that transfers of securities are registered within 14 days of notification of the transfer.

Despite this requirement, it is recommended that transfers should actually be effected within two working days of notification. If there is a high volume of trading in their securities, an issuer may want to appoint a company registrar to manage their share register for them. As well as dealing with the administration of the share register they can, for example, report on unusual transactions and the build-up of large holdings or the spread of shareholders by type and size. They can also manage the issue of notices to nominees, seeking information on beneficial owners, under s 212 of the Companies Act (see Appendix 7).

4.4 APPLICATION FOR ADMISSION

As far as the Exchange is concerned, there are very limited formalities for a company to go through in order to obtain a trading facility for its securities. There are only three procedures and a time limit to be complied with, and these are listed below.

4.4.1 Application form

Application must be made in writing on the application form published by the Stock Exchange. This is reproduced in Appendix 1.

4.4.2 Admission document

The application must be accompanied by an 'Admission Document' except for two exemptions. If the application is being made for securities of a class that is already traded on AIM, such as in the case of a rights issue or a scrip issue, then the Admission Document may not be required. Also for companies joining AIM from the Official List or from the USM there are transitional arrangements which dispense with the document.

Even in circumstances where new shares are issued of a class already traded on AIM, such as a rights issue, there may still be a requirement to produce an Admission Document. As described elsewhere, the POS Regulations permit the Exchange discretion to allow the omission of information in such circumstances.

This Admission Document is to contain the information required of a prospectus as required by the UK's Public Offer of Securities Regulations 1995 (POS Regulations), together with additional information specified by the Exchange. This information must be supplied even if the document is not sent to shareholders and does not constitute a prospectus. This will arise if new funds are not being raised nor new securities issued. It will therefore be a form of pseudo-prospectus. The intention is that there should be a document available to future investors who buy their shares in the market, that gives them information equivalent to a full prospectus. This will give them the information to make informed judgements and is seen as potentially boosting share trading after the initial issue of shares (see Chapter 5 for details of the information requirements).

4.4.3 Payment of fees

The application form and the Admission Document must be accompanied by payment of the initial admission charge. This annual fee escalates after the first year as shown below:

Admission and Year 1	£2,500
Year 2	£3,000
Year 3	£4,000

After the initial admission charge, the fee is payable on 1 January in each year. However, if admission takes place in the final quarter of the year then the second year's fee is not due until up to 15 months later. If made before this then the second year's fee may be due as little as three months after admission.

Cheques and bankers drafts should be made payable to The London Stock Exchange. Payment by telegraphic transfer can be arranged through the AIM Department of the Exchange.

Persistent non-payment of fees may result in suspension of trading.

4.4.4 Notice period

The two documents and the accompanying payment must be received by the AIM Department of the Exchange at least 72 hours before the issuer wishes the securities to be admitted to trading.

Since trading would normally begin at 8.30 in the morning, the application form and other documents need to be received by 8.30 am three days previously. The offices of the Exchange are generally open at 7.30 in the morning.

4.5 DATE OF ADMISSION

Admission of securities to be traded is not automatic but only becomes effective when the Exchange announces the fact. This allows for the exercise of discretion if there is some reason that leads the Exchange to the view that a company, its directors or controlling shareholders are not suitable. However this discretion is likely to be exercised very rarely, as evidenced by the fact that the Exchange will not review the Admission Document.

Admission will be either through the electronic information systems or by posting on the notice board at the Capel Court entrance to the Exchange building in Bartholomew Lane, London EC2N 1HP.

As stated at **4.1.1** above, it should be noted that the Exchange reserves discretion to impose further conditions before admitting a security to AIM. It would appear that any such requirement would be based upon a reading of the Admission Document or upon other information received about a company. This is a general discretion and it is not clear how it might be exercised or for what cause.

CHAPTER 5

The Admission Document

5.1 INTRODUCTION

An Admission Document is required in the form discussed below when shares are admitted to trading for the first time – when the issuer joins AIM – and in most circumstances when new shares are issued. Note that this is a summary of some of the main points of the POS Regulations that are relevant to AIM securities. It is not intended to be exhaustive and the reader should consult a lawyer or the regulations themselves for precise information.

The AIM Rules say that an Admission Document is not required when an issuer is applying for securities to be admitted to trading which are of the same class as securities that are already admitted. This apparent exemption covers rights issues, shares offered in a takeover etc. However, it carries a crucial rider: exemption is given unless the POS Regulations require a prospectus. The POS Regulations do indeed contain an exemption from publication of a prospectus as a result of shares issued during a takeover, but in the case of a rights issue (or other securities of the class already admitted and offered to existing shareholders eg a scrip issue) they only say that an authorised exchange may grant exemption. This turns the matter full circle. The exchange has, however, changed its rules to mirror the POS Regulations and automatically to allow omission of the information covered in paragraphs 41 to 47 of those regulations, which is mainly financial and historical information (described in detail below) if up-to-date, equivalent information is available to shareholders. An Admission Document will generally still be required but in most cases this will only give information on the securities being issued and summary information on the company. The result will be a much less expensive exercise, requiring less verification, than would otherwise be necessary.

An Admission Document will not be required where an AIM company issues new securities of a class already traded on AIM which satisfy a de minimis requirement and 'up-to-date equivalent information' is available. This information would have to be available from published accounts or previous Admission Documents. The de minimis test is that 'the number or estimated market value or the nominal value or, in the absence of a nominal value, the accounting par value of the securities offered amounts to less than 10% of the number or corresponding value of securities of the same class already in issue'. The issuer will still have to submit a written application to the Stock Exchange for the securities to be admitted to trading.

The AIM Regulations require that an Admission Document shall be in English. Curiously, there is no requirement for future communications with shareholders to be in English. In practice one would not imagine that overseas issuers would have any reason to exploit this omission.

5.2 ADMISSION DOCUMENT TO COMPLY WITH THE POS REGULATIONS

The Admission Document must contain the information specified under the POS Regulations whether or not a prospectus would actually be required by those regulations (Rule 16.10). The POS Regulations apply to companies raising finance by offering new shares to the public in the UK. However there are many exemptions from those regulations that mean that in many instances the Admission Document for AIM will not actually fall under them but will have the same form; it will be a pseudo-POS prospectus. In such circumstances the document may constitute an investment advertisement under the Financial Services Act 1986. There is an exemption from this also,[1] if the document contains the information required from the POS Regulations and also information 'required or permitted' by the rules of the Exchange (or another recognised exchange within the European Economic Area). This creates the curious situation

---

[1] Financial Services Act 1986 (Investment Advertisements) (Exemptions) (No 2) Order 1995.

where a document that contains extra information that is not specifically required by any authority constitutes an investment advertisement because of this extra information. The Exchange has amended its rules to remove this apparent anomaly. They now permit an issuer to include other factual information not specifically mentioned in the AIM Rules or POS Regulations where the issuer 'reasonably considers it necessary' for investors to form an informed judgement. If the document is an investment advertisement then it will need to be approved by a person authorised under the Act (see **7.3**).

The following information is required under the POS Regulations and is therefore a requirement of the AIM Admission Document.

5.2.1 Persons responsible

One of the first requirements, after saying who the issuer is, is to give details of the persons responsible for the document. This will include the directors of the offeror together with others who may have become responsible for the document under the terms of the Financial Services Act and the POS Regulations.

There are cases where the issuer of securities may not be the offeror, eg a major shareholder may offer some of their securities for sale through a public offer or placing. In such circumstances it is the offeror and its directors who are the persons responsible.

The names and addresses (home or business) of the persons responsible must be given together with their job functions.

5.2.2 Formal statement by offeror

The regulations call for a formal statement by the offeror of securities. In the case of a company issuing new shares, it will be the directors who must make this statement. However, if an existing shareholder is selling shares then it will be that shareholder, or its directors if it is a limited company, who must make the statement. Venture capitalists or other investors would therefore have to make such a statement although it may relate to matters outside their knowledge or direct control.

The statement itself must declare that 'to the best of their knowledge the information contained in the prospectus is in accordance with the facts and that the prospectus makes no omission likely to affect the import of such information' (POS Regs 1995 Sch 1 para 10).

Since the offeror will appear in the list of persons responsible for the prospectus this will attract attention to their statutory responsibility for its contents. This may further encourage such passive investors to avoid becoming offerors and to realise their investments either in the aftermarket or through a share placing, with an intermediary taking responsibility for a prospectus and subsequent sale of shares to the public.

There is also a formal statement required in the following words, 'If you are in any doubt about the contents of this document you should consult a person authorised under the Financial Services Act 1986 who specialises in advising on the acquisition of shares and debentures' or words to like effect (POS Regs 1995 Sch 1 para 8).

5.2.3 Details of the securities

The document must describe the securities being offered, including their rights regarding the following:

1 If they are shares:
   (a) voting;
   (b) dividends;
   (c) return of capital on a winding-up;
   (d) redemption.

   The document must also summarise what would be required for any of those rights to be changed.
2 If they are debentures:
   (a) interest payable;
   (b) repayment of principal.
3 If they are securities such as convertible preference shares (or warrants) that are convertible into ordinary shares or other securities:
   (a) conversion terms;
   (b) conversion dates;
   (c) how the investor can exercise conversion rights;
   (d) details of the security that they can be converted into.

4 Dates (if any) for payment of dividends or interest.
5 Procedures for exercising any pre-emption rights attaching to securities – this particularly applies to warrants and convertible securities.
6 Why the securities are being issued – for what purpose?
7 The number of securities issued and offered.
8 The total proceeds of the offer of securities, before and after the expenses of the offer.
9 The minimum amount which, in the directors' opinion, must be raised for:
   (a) the purchase of any property;
   (b) any preliminary expenses or commissions payable;
   (c) the repayment of loans used to finance any of the foregoing;
   (d) working capital.

   The sources and amounts of funding for these categories of expenditure if they are not provided from the issue.
10 The amounts of any expenses of the offer or commission payable to anyone for subscribing or procuring others to subscribe.
11 Details of any underwriting arrangements.
12 The period during which the offer is open.
13 Payment arrangements, including paying agents, timetable, what happens to moneys received during the period between application and allotment, the procedure and timetable for returning money from unsuccessful applications.

5.2.4 Details of the issuer

The following details of the issuer are required:

- name;
- address of its registered office;
- registration place and number;
- the date and place of its incorporation;
- for a non-UK company, the address of its principal place of business in the UK;
- its legal form (eg limited liability company) – if part of a group, a description of the group structure;
- summary of its objects (from its memorandum of association);
- authorised and issued share capital
  — number of shares, nominal value, amount paid up

  - details of securities convertible into shares
  - details of people or corporations who may exercise control over the issuer;
- other securities in issue.

5.2.5 Description of principal activities

The document must include a description of its principal activities. While there is no definition of what constitutes 'principal activities' we expect that this will be obvious in most cases and that it is better to err on the side of caution. It must be better to give too much information than to risk misleading investors or the Exchange through omission. Specifically the document should cover:

- information on exceptional factors that have influenced the issuer's activities;
- a statement of dependence on patents, intellectual property rights or contracts where these are fundamental to the business;
- information on significant investments in progress;
- information on legal or arbitration proceedings (in progress, pending or threatened) which may have a significant impact on the business.

5.2.6 Accounting information

Financial information on the issuer may be provided on a consolidated basis, rather than having to include information on each separate subsidiary, if their inclusion would not provide significant extra information. The issuer may choose to include either (POS Regs 1995 para 45):

- the previous three years' accounts; or
- an accountant's report covering the three years.

The latter alternative of an accountant's report may be preferable when there have been significant changes to the form of the company or to accounting policies or where there has been a change of auditor during the period.

If the issuer has not been in existence for three years then the financial information must be provided for those periods when it was produced.

If the latest financial period ended within three months of the proposed issue of securities and accounts have not yet been prepared at the issue date then the requirement for them or for an accountant's report does not apply to the period. However, this financial period would then be covered by the requirement below for interim accounts or an accountant's report.

If the issue of securities takes place more than nine months after the latest financial year-end then either interim accounts or an interim report must be included. They must cover a period ending not more than three months before the issue date. Broadly the same additional information given below for the three-year period applies to this interim period, with the differences noted. Interim accounts do not need to be audited but must be prepared to the same standard as year-end accounts.

If interim accounts have been published which do not satisfy the requirement above then they must, nonetheless, be included. For example, this may apply if they related to a period that ended more than three months before the issue date or if they have not been prepared to the required standard. There must, in such circumstances, be three items of information accompanying them:

- explanation of the purpose for which the accounts were prepared;
- reference to legislation under which they were prepared;
- the name and address of the person responsible for them, that person's consent to their inclusion and acceptance of responsibility for them.

The consent of persons responsible for accounts prepared in the past could conceivably cause problems if accountants who prepared interim accounts were reluctant to take responsibility for the purposes of a prospectus (see **6.4**). This part of the regulations does not provide for an alternative to consent, such as an explanation of why the accountants do not want to take responsibility or an accountant's report instead of such consent. Anyone contemplating issuing a prospectus must therefore be mindful of these issues before publishing any interim accounts.

The additional requirements referred to are as follows:

1 *When the document includes accounts*:

(a) A statement from the directors (note this means all of the directors) saying that the accounts have been prepared in accordance with the law and taking responsibility for them, or explaining why they cannot make the statement.

(b) Name and address of the auditors, a copy of their audit reports and their consent to the inclusion of these reports in the document. They must also accept responsibility for the reports, which extends their liability to potential investors from their original responsibility which is only to the company. They must also confirm that they have not become aware of anything that renders their original reports invalid. If they are unable to make this statement then they must give their reasons.

An auditor's disclaimer to previous audit reports may not prevent a company from raising new funds as long as the reasons for the disclaimer do not point to a continuing material uncertainty regarding the company's financial condition. The reasons for the disclaimer must also not create doubt about the future prospects for the company.

(c) For interim accounts there is no requirement for a statement from the directors but a similar requirement for one from the person responsible for preparing those interim accounts. This is supplemented by the consent of that person for the interim accounts to be included.

2 *When the document includes an accountant's report*: The alternative of an accountant's report must be provided by someone qualified to act as an auditor. It does not require an accompanying statement from the directors of the company. It does require the name and address of the person responsible for the report and (if it is different) the name and address of those responsible for auditing the accounts on which the report is based. The person making the report must give formal consent to its inclusion in the document and must take responsibility for it. The person must also confirm that the report gives a 'true and fair view of the state of affairs and profit or loss of the issuer'. The regulations provide an alternative, for a prospectus to include an explanation of why this statement cannot be given. However, it is hard to think of circumstances where this would be acceptable to potential investors.

5.2.7 Prospects

The document must refer to the prospects for the business, though a profit forecast is not required. Indeed, since an accountant's report would be required on a profit forecast, many issuers will try hard to avoid using any form of words that might be held to constitute a forecast, albeit inadvertently. For example, a statement that sales were expected to double during the forthcoming year might enable someone to calculate what the likely resulting profit would be: this would therefore constitute a profit forecast.

Prospects are therefore often likely to be described in general terms and the POS Regulations require that these should cover any significant recent trends (since the last year-end) and that prospects should be discussed for – at least – the current financial year.

Significant acquisitions or disposals since the end of the previous financial year would be covered under these requirements.

Note that some issuers may wish to publish a profit forecast in order to assist their marketing of shares.

5.2.8 Matters not required

The fact that the POS Regulations are less demanding than requirments for the Official List will save some legal time and effort. The absence of a requirement for a statement on working capital is not very significant because it is required by the AIM Rules. However, there is no requirement for:

- a statement of indebtedness;
- a summary of material contracts;
- a summary of the Articles of Association;
- a history of share capital.

Neither the AIM Rules nor the POS Regulations call for such documents relating to material contracts to be displayed to the public for 14 days, as required for the Official List.

5.2.9 General duty of disclosure

There is a requirement for a prospectus to contain 'all such information as investors would reasonably require and reasonably expect to find there for the purpose of making an informed assessment . . .' (POS Regs 1995 para 9). Will this general duty lead to legal advisers calling for the inclusion of all these matters not specified by the POS Regulations? It is hoped that it will not have this effect, which would result in increasing the cost and complication associated with AIM with little clear benefit to investors.

5.2.10 Omission of information

The POS Regulations provide for information to be omitted in certain circumstances:

1. If disclosure would be contrary to the public interest (by application to the Treasury).
2. Where the offeror is not the issuer and the information required to be published under the regulations is not available to him, despite making reasonable efforts to obtain it. Quite what constitutes 'reasonable efforts' is not clear. It is very unlikely that a shareholder will offer securities through AIM (that were not previously traded in this way) without the agreement and support of the issuer of those securities. However it has happened on the Official List and this provision of the POS Regulations removes one of the barriers.
3. For information of minor importance, or which poses a serious detriment to the issuer and where the omission would not be misleading (by application to the Exchange, which is expected to be authorised by the Treasury to give such derogation).
4. Shares may be offered to existing shareholders through a rights issue without the publication of a full POS prospectus (see **5.1** above).
5. Information that is inappropriate to the issuer's sphere of activity, its legal form or to the securities to which the prospectus relates, may be omitted.
6. If a prospectus has been published within the previous 12 months then only the differences need to be published together with a reference to the previous document. However, in practice it may be just as easy to produce a new document.
7. There is a 'small issue' provision which allows the Exchange to authorise an issue of new shares without a prospectus if they account

for less than 10% of the market value, number or par value etc of the shares in issue.

5.3 ADDITIONAL INFORMATION REQUIRED BY THE EXCHANGE

There are a number of items of information, in addition to those specified under the POS Regulations, that the Exchange demands should be included in an Admission Document and these are detailed below.

5.3.1 A working capital statement

There must be a statement by the issuer that in the opinion of the directors, after having made due and careful enquiry, the working capital available to the issuer and its group is sufficient for present requirements. This is required regardless of whether new finance is being raised or the company is just seeking a market to allow its shares to be traded.

Directors of a company that issues a prospectus containing a misleading or incorrect statement that is negligently made may be personally liable for losses that an investor may incur (POS Regulations 1995). This statement should not, therefore, be made without considerable care.

The adviser and corporate broker will advise on what constitutes 'due and careful enquiry'. These terms are not defined in the document or in law but are decided by custom and practice and with regard to what is reasonable in each case. We would expect the issuer to have drawn up a cash flow forecast as follows:

1 Extending for at least 12 months and, depending upon the nature of the business, a period of 18 or 24 months might be appropriate. This would be expected to show that existing bank facilities are sufficient during the period and that there is no indication that they will deteriorate immediately after the forecast period.

   The figures should generally be done on a monthly basis for at least the first 12 months, particularly if there are significant seasonal fluctuations in the business. Depending upon the circumstances, quarterly figures might be sufficient after that. There should be some work done to establish the degree of fluctuation within the month or quarter. If there were wide fluctuations it would be necessary to identify the maximum borrowing requirement in each period.

2 With clearly stated assumptions on which the forecast is based which have been carefully considered and are reasonable in all the circumstances. To support the forecast, there should be calculations of the effect of variations in the assumptions. These should cover the range of outcomes that a reasonable person might believe to be possible.

3 Dealing with any banking facilities that expire within the period covered by the forecast. In such circumstances the issuer should have obtained a letter of comfort from their bankers. This should state when overdraft or other facilities expire and that at the present date they can see no reason why these should not be renewed in the ordinary course of business.

If the cash flow forecast indicates that there may be insufficient working capital within the period it covers, then there are often actions that can be taken which will allow the necessary statement to be made in the Admission Document eg:

- reduce discretionary capital expenditure;
- seek further bank finance;
- raise more money from shareholders.

The directors of the issuer take responsibility for the working capital statement. This is unlike the Official List, where the sponsor must write to the Stock Exchange. While there is no requirement for anyone other than the issuer to take responsibility for the working capital statement, it would be surprising if the adviser and broker did not wish to see the documents supporting it and to satisfy themselves that, on the face of it, they were reasonable.

There is no specific Stock Exchange requirement to have a reporting accountant's review of the supporting documentation to a working capital statement. However, unless it is quite obvious beyond a shadow of doubt that working capital will be sufficient for the foreseeable future, we would expect an issuer to obtain such a report. Indeed the AIM Rules do require the nominated adviser to have satisfied itself that the directors have instigated a suitable verification/due diligence process. Discussions with potential institutional investors in AIM suggest that they would normally expect an accountant's report to support the statement. The extent of these checks and enquiries is important to the company seeking to join AIM; on the one hand they lead to expense but on the other hand they provide comfort to both investors and to directors who are under a statutory duty to avoid making reckless or misleading statements.

5.3.2 Support for any profit forecast (Rule 16.11.b)

If the document contains a profit forecast then it must also contain further information and support (detailed below). The Exchange may deem words to constitute a profit forecast even though that was not the intention of the issuer and the word 'profit' is not used, so considerable care must be taken over the wording. The circumstances that may be deemed to constitute a forecast include:

1 Any form of words that state expressly or imply a level or likely level of profits (or losses) for a period after the last published audited accounts. For example, a statement that current year profits are likely to be at a similar level to the previous year's, would constitute a profit forecast.
2 Data from which a calculation may be made indicating an approximate figure for future profits or losses. For example, data on industry growth which is expected by the directors might permit an investor to apply this to the turnover of the issuer and to calculate an increase in sales and profits that might result.

If a profit forecast is made, the document must contain both of the following:

1 A statement by the issuer that the forecast has been made after due and careful enquiry by the issuer (Rule 16.11.b.i).
2 A report on the forecast by the issuer's auditors or reporting accountants employed for the purpose (Rule 16.11.b.ii). That accountant's report must confirm that the forecast has been properly compiled on the basis stated, which is consistent with the accounting policies of the issuer, and it must include a statement of the principal assumptions on which the forecast is based.

In fact the assumptions refer to the degree of risk or uncertainty that is outside the direct control of the directors. The assumptions to be stated are only those that relate to matters outside the control of the directors and which could have a material effect on the achievement of the forecast. Therefore the price charged for a product or service would probably not be disclosed but the purchase price for essential raw materials might be, while interest, tax and inflation rates generally would be. The directors of the issuer should not be able to claim afterwards that they disclosed a risk and that shareholders understood it when, in fact, that risk was something they should or could have been able to control.

It must be made clear to which particular aspect of the forecast the stated assumptions relate and the measure of uncertainty that attaches to them.

5.3.3 Wording

On the first page of the document, there must be the following words:

> 'Application has been/{will be} made for these securities to be admitted to trading on the Alternative Investment Market of the London Stock Exchange (AIM). It is emphasised that no application is being made for admission of these securities to the Official List.
>
> AIM is a market designed primarily for emerging or smaller companies. The rules of this market are less demanding than those of the Official List. The Exchange has not itself examined this document.'

5.3.4 Information on the directors of the issuer

The information on directors that is required in the Admission Document is as follows:

1. Their directorships over the previous five years.
2. Any unspent convictions.
3. Details of personal bankruptcies.
4. Details of receiverships or liquidations.

— The details of receiverships or liquidations are required for companies where the director of the issuer was a director at the time of the event or within the 12 months before it.

5 Any public criticisms of a director by statutory or regulatory authorities.

— Public criticism refers to published reports of DTI investigators, as well as reports by liquidators or receivers. It would also include censure by the Stock Exchange or professional bodies of which the director was a member.

5.3.5 Details of promoters

A promoter is someone who seeks to raise funds for an enterprise. It has been defined by the courts as someone who 'undertakes to form a company with reference to a given project and to set it going and who takes the necessary steps to accomplish that purpose'. The definition will include individuals but may also include venture capital firms who establish a management buy-out vehicle or holding company that establishes a company in order to provide a vehicle to sell off a part of its business. In this context a promoter includes someone who has acted in this capacity during a two-year period leading up to the application for admission but does not apply to those who advise or act as brokers to the AIM issue. The Admission Document must give details of any such promoters. The key date for measuring the two-year period would be the date on which the application for admission was delivered to the Exchange.

There are three items of information on any promoters which must be published in the Admission Document:

1 *Their names and addresses:* addresses published may be business rather than home addresses.
2 *Details of their relationship with the issuer and advisers*: advisers, in this context, means nominated advisers for the issue, nominated brokers and other advisers. This ensures that any commission or benefit earned by anyone associated with the promotion of a company is publicly disclosed. It would, for example, be necessary to disclose whether the promoters were partners, shareholders or blood relations of the issuer, its directors or advisers.

3 *Details of any payment or other benefit*: payments or benefits that have been or will be received by promoters must be disclosed to the extent required by the law. This will cover, for example, shares given in payment, a right to subscribe for shares at a preferential price, benefits in kind etc.

5.3.6 Details of advisers

The Admission Document must contain the name and address of the nominated adviser and the nominated broker. These roles can be carried out by the same firm.

5.3.7 Details of substantial shareholders

A substantial shareholder is one who is entitled to exercise 10% or more of the votes at a general meeting of the issuer. This requirement therefore relates to control of the issuer. It does not apply to a 'bare trustee'.

The names and percentage shareholding of all substantial shareholders must be included in the Admission Document.

The requirement is broadened in a number of ways to include those who were entitled to exercise this voting percentage:

1 *Within 12 months of the application for admission*: the wording in the regulations appears to cover even those who have now sold their shares.
2 *On substantially all matters at a general meeting*: the difference between 'all' and 'substantially all' is not defined and is a matter for judgement. It is hard to foresee circumstances where the difference would cause any practical problems.
3 *In relation to a subsidiary, parent or fellow subsidiary of the issuer*: it is hard to discern the reason for this requirement to disclose a substantial shareholding in a sister company that simply has the same parent as the issuer. However it is a clear requirement of the rules.

   The term 'parent' is defined in the Companies Act 1985 s 258. It would refer to a substantial shareholder (not necessarily with more than 50% voting control) whose instructions would generally be followed by the directors of the issuer. It would also apply to a company having voting control of the issuer.

5.4 SUPPLEMENTARY DOCUMENT

There are occasions when new information will come to light or circumstances may change materially after the publication of an Admission Document but before the securities have been admitted to trading on AIM. Perhaps:

- a significant inaccuracy comes to light; or
- there is a significant change or new matter that arises.

For example, this could refer to a material contract cancelled, a fraud coming to light, a change in tax legislation etc. The test is whether the regulations would have required the inclusion of the information if it had been known earlier. It is 'significant' if it could have influenced an informed assessment by an investor.

An offeror of securities is required by the POS Regulations (POS Regs 1995 para 10) to issue a supplementary prospectus correcting the inaccuracy or including the new information. The AIM Rules require a supplementary document to be published in these circumstances even if the POS Regulations do not apply.

5.5 RECENT PROSPECTUS

When a full prospectus has been published within 12 months preceding the admission of securities to AIM, the POS Regulations (POS Regs 1995 para 8(6)) provide for publication of a prospectus that includes the previous document and contains the differences from it. This applies whether the previous prospectus related to the same or a different class of securities. By extension, this applies also to the Admission Document to AIM. However, in practice there is likely to be no more work in producing a completely new document, indeed the documentation of differences could be very complex. This provision is unlikely to be utilised unless new securities are issued very shortly after a previous issue, perhaps as a result of an acquisition opportunity.

5.6 VERIFICATION/DUE DILIGENCE

Verification is the process of checking a public document to ensure that it is accurate and not misleading. Directors take legal responsibility for a document that is distributed to the public with a view to raising funds. They may be liable to compensate shareholders who incur a loss due to a negligent misstatement and there is also a possibility of criminal liability (see **6.4**).

Because of this and because the company's nominated broker and nominated adviser invest their reputation in an Admission Document they will insist on a process of verification for it. The degree of verification may be less if the document is not circulated to the public but the broker and adviser would still wish to be confident that it is factually correct. The requirements are of a legal nature and are not an Exchange requirement.

To verify a document the company's lawyers will highlight every individual statement of fact or opinion and will seek some evidence to support each of them. This may be supplied by records from the business, experts' reports, data published from a reliable source or other documents in the public domain. Even newspaper reports may be acceptable, depending upon the circumstances and the degree to which an investment decision may be influenced by the statement. It is not generally sufficient to respond that a point is common knowledge; documentary evidence must usually be put forward. If the directors are offering their opinion then the document should state clearly that the matter is an opinion eg The directors believe . . . etc. Even an opinion must be reasonably held, so some support is helpful. Occasionally the directors may be able to state an opinion supported only by their experience in the business.

The term due diligence relates to the use of such due diligence to make enquiries and investigations in order to ensure that a public document is not misleading and to satisfy authorities, such as the Exchange, that a company is suitable for Listing. Of course AIM does not have any requirement for a sponsor to report on suitability. Nonetheless, the term relates to a broad process of investigation of which the verification procedure forms a part. A long form report, described below, is the written output of the due diligence carried out for a company to obtain admission to the Official List or the USM.

5.7 A LONG FORM REPORT

A long form report has no technical definition but the term relates to a body of custom and practice. It refers to 'a detailed report [prepared by accountants] covering various aspects of the company's business including its management, profit record, assets and liabilities and its prospects'. (Auditing Guideline, Prospectuses and the Reporting Accountant – Feb 1986.) It is prepared for sponsors to companies joining the Official List in order to satisfy them in respect of their duty to inform the Exchange of any matters that should be brought to the Exchange's attention and to provide them with comfort with regard to their statutory responsibilities in taking responsibility for the prospectus, albeit that they have extensive indemnities from the issuer and its directors. It is sometimes argued that the report also provides comfort for the directors of the issuer who also have statutory responsibilities. We believe that the long form report might provide real comfort to directors and prospective shareholders if it combined more of a commercial review of the business with a review of financial systems and accounts. This might be on the basis of joint or co-reporting with expert advisers. However we believe the current approach often concentrates too much on historic figures to be truly helpful in examining future prospects and risks which, together with the adequacy of financial controls, are what concern investors.

The report is discussed in outline here because some nominated advisers may want to have one prepared. Since the cost is generally in excess of £20,000 and often much higher, it is clearly highly relevant to directors thinking of obtaining a trading facility on AIM.

There is no set format for the report, which will be different for every business. Its content should be agreed between the sponsor, issuer and the reporting accountant.

5.7.1 Typical engagement letter

Set out below is a list of the main headings and issues that would be covered in the engagement letter from the accountants, which is generally addressed jointly to the issuer and sponsor (adviser):

1 The long form report

1 Period covered (generally five years up to the last balance sheet date).
2 General purpose of the report (ie that it is a detailed report on the business and its financial position).
3 Review of the effect of the company's strategy on its future performance.
4 Review of trends disclosed by current trading results.
5 Commentary on the company's medium term prospects, with particular reference to the following:
   (a) management forecasts for the next two years;
   (b) past forecasting accuracy including current performance against budget;
   (c) the principal assumptions underlying the forecasts – their vulnerability and the effect of varying key assumptions.
6 Commentary on pro forma forecast profit & loss account, balance sheet and cash flow forecast. This will include confirmation that accounting policies are appropriate and that no material changes are anticipated.

2 The short form report

The short form report covers the financial information to be included in the Admission Document.

3 Letter of comfort to directors regarding their working capital statement

The directors' working capital statement is their own responsibility but the report will include a letter of comfort. This will review how reasonable the underlying assumptions are and the mathematical accuracy of the calculations.

4 Other matters

Other matters dealt with in the report will include:

1 Letter of comfort, to the directors and their advisers, regarding the accuracy of numbers included in the prospectus.

2 A review of the auditors' annual management letters to the directors regarding the company's systems and controls.

The engagement letter will generally ask the directors to prepare forecasts and to prepare a detailed description of the company's financial procedures. It will also request the reporting accountant's attendance at drafting meetings for the prospectus. It will invariably exclude liability to all parties other than the directors and the sponsors to whom the letter is addressed.

The tenor of the long form report, as discussed above, is that it approaches the business from a financial perspective rather than from one of commercial due diligence. It would be unusual, therefore, for the reporting accountants to examine commercial market reports or published articles, ring suppliers, customers and industry observers or to carry out company searches in order to produce a commentary on the market structure, competition and prospects. If an issuer and their advisers agree to conduct a broader commercial due diligence then they may instruct the reporting accountants or they may use management consultants to provide a separate report.

Typical headings for the long form report itself are as follows:

- executive summary;
- history of the business;
- the industry and marketplace;
- how the business works;
- regulation;
- competitors;
- customers;
- business overview;
- trading results (five years);
- summary of performance;
- significant issues;
- seasonality/volatility;
- exceptional items;
- pensions;
- taxation;
- net assets;
- cash flow;
- historical trading;

- management and financial reporting controls;
- taxation.

5.8 PUBLICATION OF ADMISSION DOCUMENT

If an Admission Document constitutes a prospectus under the Public Offer of Securities Regulations 1995 then a copy must be delivered to the registrar of companies for registration (POS Regs para 4). This must take place before publication of the prospectus and will normally be done when the document is delivered to the Exchange.

The regulations provide for penalties for non-compliance of up to two years' imprisonment or a fine or both.

A company may join AIM through an introduction of its existing shares without raising new investment. In that case the Admission Document is not a prospectus and there is no requirement to send it to existing investors. Nonetheless, it must be published so that it is available for future investors to consult. The Admission Document must be made available, free of charge, at an address in the UK that is stated in the document. The minimum period during which the document is made available is 14 days from the date of admission to AIM.

In practice, a company that wants to raise funds will use its Admission Document to do so. It will therefore wish to make the document available for longer than the minimum time in order to get the best possible response. Even if funds are not raised immediately on joining AIM, the document may be a valuable public relations tool.

CHAPTER 6

Duties and responsibilities of directors

The duties and responsibilities of directors of an issuer are set out in the AIM Rules, the Companies Act 1985, the Financial Services Act 1986 and the POS Regulations 1995. (Those relating to insider dealing are discussed in Chapter 11.)

6.1 ACCEPTANCE OF RESPONSIBILITY

The directors must accept responsibility, both collectively and individually, for compliance with the rules applying to AIM (Rule 16.8).

The form in which this shall be done is not specified in the AIM Rules but we suggest it should be effected through:

1 *Board resolution* – this should be duly minuted and should include provisions:
   (a) adopting the Model Code (or more stringent requirements) for share dealings (see Chapter 10)
      — this should apply to all directors and also to any employees who are not directors but who are likely to have unpublished, price sensitive information
      — this should apply to directors and employees of the issuer itself but also those of a subsidiary or parent
      — any person who has unpublished price sensitive information must, in any case, comply with legislation on insider dealing

- when discussing such unpublished price sensitive information with a third party adviser, they should be told that they are being given confidential price sensitive information. The commonly used form of words that is used is, 'you are now an insider';

(b) undertaking to follow the published rules of AIM.

2 *Directors' undertakings* – directors should individually indicate their understanding of their obligations through personal letters to the company or company secretary.

6.2 NOTIFICATION OF DIRECTORS' INTERESTS

Responsibility for notifying the Exchange of changes in directors' interests falls on both the issuer and the directors concerned.

The directors are bound to disclose details of their own interests and those of 'connected persons' (see Glossary for definition) to the issuer. They give an undertaking to the issuer to this effect (Rule 16.9.a) in the Admission Document or on appointment as directors. They are also bound to do this by ss 324, 325(3) or (4) and 328 of the Companies Act 1985.

The director is required to undertake to disclose information about share dealings of connected parties to the issuer within five working days of becoming aware of it (Rule 16.9.a).

6.3 NEW COMPANIES

Directors and employees of a 'new business' must undertake not to dispose of any interest in AIM securities for one year following admission. This may apply not only to any securities issued when the company first joins AIM but also to subsequent secondary issues – such as a rights issue. A new business is one that is independent and has not been earning revenue (income from sales, fees or commissions) from its main business for at least two years. It is important to note that a company will not be considered as having a two-year track record merely by virtue of buying a peripheral business that has a sufficient track record. For example, consider a business that has been trading for one year, joins AIM and raises money at that time from the issue of new shares and, six months later, issues further new shares (also admitted to trading on AIM). The directors and employees must undertake not to dispose of their securities for 12 months from each issue of shares.

This requirement applies only to directors and employees at the time of admission, those joining afterwards are not bound to comply. Nor does this restriction apply to connected persons, although they would have to abide by the restrictions applying to close periods and the director's possession of unpublished price sensitive information (see **10.4**).

There are only three exemptions from this requirement:

- in the event of a court order requiring disposal eg the result of bankruptcy or a matrimonial settlement;
- a takeover being declared unconditional;
- the death of the director or employee.

There are no exceptions for financial need nor to permit the transfer of shares within a family or to family trusts.

6.4 RESPONSIBILITY FOR A PROSPECTUS

The Exchange places responsibility for the Admission Document clearly on the directors of the issuer and in addition there is a legal duty placed on directors when this document is also a prospectus. It is important, particularly for professional advisers, to note that they, as well as directors of an issuer, may be responsible for part or all of a prospectus and will have legal liability for the part for which they have responsibility. A person is responsible for all or part of a prospectus when they accept responsibility (eg provide expert reports) or where they are the offeror (or a director of the offeror) of securities (POS Regs para 13). The persons responsible have to accept responsibility and their names will appear in the prospectus.

6.4.1 Sanctions

There are three types of sanction against directors and others who are in dereliction of their responsibilities: to pay compensation under provisions of the Financial Services Act 1986; a legal liability under contract law; and criminal liability. These are looked at in more detail below.

Compensation

The Public Offer of Securities Regulations (paragraph 14) specify that a person who is responsible for a prospectus is liable to pay compensation to any person who has acquired securities and incurred a loss. This applies if the loss results from an 'untrue or misleading statement' or from 'the omission . . . of any matter' that 'investors would reasonably require . . . for the purpose of making an informed assessment'.

The directors of the issuer are not only responsible for compensating people who suffer a loss following subscription for shares as a result of a prospectus but also those who buy their shares subsequently. The plaintiff would have no need to show that they relied on the prospectus, only that it was reckless or misleading and that they suffered a loss.

There are a number of defences against a plaintiff that a person responsible for the prospectus can put forward:

1 The prime defence is that at the time '. . . he reasonably believed, having made such enquiries . . . as were reasonable, that the statement was true and not misleading or that . . . [a matter] . . . was properly omitted . . .'.
2 That 'he believed on reasonable grounds' that an expert's statement was included with that person's consent and that the person was competent.
3 That he acted to publish a correction as soon as he became aware of an error or omission.
4 That a statement by an 'official person' was accurately reproduced.
5 That a person acquiring the securities did so with knowledge of the error or omission.
6 That he reasonably believed that the change, new matter or inaccuracy did not require a supplementary prospectus ie was too trivial.

Contractual liability

If the issue of securities is underwritten, or if it is distributed through a placing, the directors will be parties to the contract with the underwriters and will therefore have liabilities under the warranties and indemnities that they enter into.

Criminal liability

Criminal liability can arise under s 47 of the Financial Services Act 1986, in respect of a director making false, misleading or reckless statements or other conduct that creates a false or misleading impression. The penalty may be a fine or imprisonment.

Some sections of the Companies Act 1985 which provide criminal penalties for misstatements are repealed and replaced under the POS Regulations 1995.

There have been very few criminal prosecutions for prospectus offences because there are more effective alternatives. If the prospectus offences are fraudulent then there are powers to prosecute under the Theft Act. The advisers to the issuer may face penalties from the self regulating organisation to which they belong and there are rights to return of money and compensation under the Financial Services Act.

6.5 SUMMARY OF DIRECTORS' STATEMENTS

Directors must make a number of statements which are specified in various places within the regulations. They must:

- accept responsibility for compliance with the rules of AIM (see **6.1**);
- take responsibility for the Admission Document (see **5.2.2**);
- take responsibility for any accounts included in the Admission Document (see **5.2.6**);
- issue a working capital statement to be included in the Admission Document (see **5.3.1**).

They will also, as a matter of practice, be required to give various undertakings and indemnities to their advisers. These will include indemnities in respect of any incorrect statements made to those advisers which they have relied upon.

CHAPTER 7

Advisers and brokers

The issuer of securities must appoint a nominated adviser and a nominated broker. Nominated advisers must be chosen from a list maintained by the Exchange while a nominated broker will be a member firm of the Exchange.

The roles can be combined, with a nominated broker also acting as a nominated adviser for an issuer if it is on the approved list maintained by the Exchange. The member firm of the Exchange must have satisfied the Exchange that it is 'competent to discharge the duties of a nominated adviser' (see **7.6** below).

7.1 CHANGE IN NOMINATED ADVISER OR BROKER

If the nominated adviser or nominated broker resigns or ceases to act for any other reason and is not replaced immediately then trading in the issuer's shares will be suspended. If there is no replacement within one month then the securities will be delisted and a new application for admission will have to be made. This will require a new Admission Document.

The Exchange advises that arrangements with a nominated adviser and a nominated broker should include a notice period of at least one month to allow time for the issuer to find a replacement.

7.2 NOTIFICATION OF CHANGES

The Exchange must be notified 'without delay' of the resignation, dismissal or change in nominated broker or nominated adviser (Rule 16.19.h). The term 'without delay' would be taken to mean a day or maybe even two but not longer. Both the issuer and the nominated adviser/broker have a responsibility to inform the Exchange.

7.3 DUTIES OF NOMINATED ADVISER

The nominated adviser may agree with the issuer to carry out duties and bear responsibilities that are additional to those required by the Exchange. They may also be obliged to take on extra responsibility due to the structure of the transaction (see **7.3.2** below)

The primary duties of the nominated adviser are to the Exchange, though other responsibilities that it may enter into are discussed in para **7.3.2** below.

7.3.1 Duties owed by the nominated adviser to the Exchange

(1) *To confirm to the Exchange that directors of a new issuer that is producing an Admission Document have received 'advice and guidance' on what their responsibilities and obligations are to comply with the Rules relating to AIM.*

Neither this rule nor (2) below apply where a company is not producing an Admission Document eg where it is joining AIM from the USM.

(2) *To confirm to the Exchange that all relevant requirements of the AIM Rules have been complied with.*

The wording of this rule is 'to the best of the knowledge and belief of the nominated adviser'. This is a lesser standard than that demanded from a sponsor to the Official List, who must also make 'due and careful enquiry' that the issuer has complied with the requirements of the listing rules. The difference means that the nominated adviser need not necessarily itself take charge of the due diligence exercise as long as it ensures that the directors of the issuer have instituted satisfactory procedures (the belief of the adviser must be reasonably held).

This rule also includes wording that specifically excludes the nominated adviser from having to take responsibility for the issuer's compliance with Regulation 9 of the POS Regulations. Regulation 9 requires that a prospectus (and the Exchange applies the same information to be included in an Admission Document) contains '. . . all such information as investors would reasonably require . . . [to make] . . . an informed assessment of (a) the assets and liabilities, financial position, profits and losses and prospects of the issuer . . . and (b) the rights attaching to these securities.'.

The purpose of this exclusion is to relieve the nominated adviser of a duty to make searching enquiry for any other matters that investors should be informed of. They must still, however, confirm that the issuer has met the specific reporting requirements of the Exchange. This means that the long form report that sponsors customarily commission (and issuers pay for) in connection with the Official List, may not be necessary for AIM. This report, discussed in **5.7**, is primarily produced to protect the sponsor when taking statutory responsibility for a prospectus.

This rule relieves the nominated adviser of responsibilities which should, in turn, reduce the cost to the issuer. However, our research suggests that some nominated advisers may still seek to apply the same standards to AIM as to the Official List, with a view to protecting their own reputation.

A further, serious complication may arise when the Admission Document actually constitutes an investment advertisement rather than coming under the POS Regulations. This may occur when shares are sold to an institution which then becomes the offeror, selling them on to investors. Such a mechanism is commonly used when one of the shareholders who is selling shares will not take responsibility for a prospectus. In these cases the rules of the nominated adviser's self regulating organisation apply. For example, the rules of the Securities and Futures Authority asks its members to 'apply appropriate expertise and to be able to show on reasonable grounds that the advertisement is fair and not misleading'. Such cases may lead to a greater degree of due diligence being applied when an Admission Document is not a POS prospectus than when it is.

(3) *To confirm to the Exchange that it will be available 'at all times' to advise and guide the directors on their continuing responsibilities and obligations to ensure compliance by the issuer with the AIM Rules.*

This use of the word 'ensure' in this rule is interesting in that it would seem to imply that the nominated adviser has a policing role on behalf of the Exchange to make sure that the issuer complies with the AIM Rules. In practical terms it cannot 'ensure' but only do its best to advise and guide the directors. Indeed the passive phrasing of being 'available' shows that the Exchange does not expect the nominated adviser to ensure that the issuer's directors seek its advice at all times. Nonetheless, use of the word ensure carries an implication that the nominated adviser would be called to account by the Exchange if it were unsuccessful in achieving compliance. In practice the nominated adviser will not be held responsible for every action a company takes but it will have a responsibility for its clients' conduct as a whole.

(4) *To confirm to the Exchange when it ceases to be the nominated adviser to the issuer.*

The nominated adviser and the issuer are therefore under separate obligations to inform the Exchange of the ending of their relationship.

While these duties may appear very limited, the Exchange does expect the nominated adviser to satisfy itself that an appropriate verification exercise has been carried out on the Admission Document. The nominated adviser may also want extra work to be done to satisfy itself as to the bona fides and prospects for the issuer. Indeed the rules that the Exchange applies to the nominated adviser carry an implication that they bear some responsibility for the conduct of their clients. While a nominated adviser may not be called to account for a single errant client, repeated misdemeanours by one or more would seem to suggest that it was failing in its responsibilities.

The level of investigatory work will depend upon the nature of the issuer. If the issuer is not seeking new funds (eg a company presently traded under Rule 4.2 of the Stock Exchange) then a lesser level of work may be necessary than for one seeking new funds. Also a company that has been trading for a long time, with a long-serving management team and with demonstrable stability, may require less work than one that is new or loss making and trading in high risk markets. A company with many subsidiaries engaged in different activities in different markets may require more work than a company with one activity in one market.

The level of investigatory work carried out will also depend upon the investment community. If investors, after enquiry, prove unwilling to provide finance for companies that have not carried out a large scale due diligence then this will become necessary for AIM, as it is for the Official List. However, the evidence from companies traded under Rule 4.2 of the Stock Exchange is that investors have been willing to put substantial sums into smaller companies which have been subject to a lesser degree of investigation. The experience of several companies on the Official List producing profit warnings shortly after raising new finance has not led to great investor confidence in the nature of some of the due diligence processes that have become customary.

Concern has been expressed about the relatively high cost associated with flotation on the Official List, much of which is associated with the legal and financial investigation process. This may turn out to be far less of a problem for AIM than has been feared because smaller companies are likely to have simpler structures and their investigation may involve less work.

The adviser will also need regular meetings with the issuer and to be given all relevant information to enable them to give continuing advice. This would cover plans for acquisitions, disposals, significant trading issues, share transactions by directors and connected parties and any other matters that might materially affect the share price. The Exchange sees the continuing role of nominated advisers as essentially reactive rather than proactive, being available to advise. Clearly, if this were an active role in management then that could bring an unwanted legal responsibility to the adviser as a shadow director.

7.3.2 Other duties into which nominated advisers may enter into

Although the Exchange's intention is clearly that the nominated adviser should be protected from legal liability for the contents of an AIM Admission Document, the role played by the nominated adviser in bringing a company to AIM may result in him becoming a 'responsible person' under the POS Regulations. There may also be instances where a nominated adviser may voluntarily take responsibility for the document in the role of a sponsor. In all such circumstances the nominated adviser will wish to satisfy himself fully that the Admission Document has been properly compiled.

This also covers circumstances where the nominated adviser becomes a responsible person by virtue of selling shares. This will occur if some existing shareholders are asked to sell shares as part of the flotation and, while assenting, decline to take responsibility for the prospectus. An example of this problem is venture capital institutions who often decline to take responsibility for a prospectus. They argue that they are investors and are not actively involved in management and cannot therefore accept legal liability for the accuracy of the prospectus that depends on knowledge of day-to-day management. This problem will require the shares to be sold to a third party who, as principal, will then sell them to investors, thereby taking responsibility for the prospectus.

In the situations referred to above, the responsible person is subject to Regulation 9 of the POS Regulations which is discussed in **7.3.1** above.

7.3.3 Providing the Exchange with such information as it may require

This clause in the rules is extremely wide and falls within the absolute discretion of the Exchange. The purpose of the clause is to provide the Exchange with powers to obtain information in the many circumstances that cannot be defined in a rule book. Examples might range from an investigation following unusual share price movements to suspicions of undisclosed transactions with directors, or late announcement of price sensitive information. It is not the intention of the Exchange to be unreasonable but to be in a position to obtain information it may need to carry out its regulatory duties.

7.4 DIFFERENCES BETWEEN A NOMINATED ADVISER AND A SPONSOR

Companies joining the Official List are required to have a sponsor who undertakes certain duties that are additional to those specified for the nominated adviser on AIM. These include:

- Reporting to the Exchange that 'all relevant matters regarding suitability for admission' have been drawn to its attention.

This is one of the reasons behind the, so-called, long form report which sponsors commission on companies they are backing (see **5.7**). There is no suitability criterion for companies to join AIM.

- Reporting to the Exchange, under the listing particulars requirements, on the:
  (a) adequacy of financial reporting procedures;
  (b) working capital statement;
  (c) profit forecast.

However there is an additional duty placed upon a nominated adviser who is required to give continuing advice and guidance to the issuer after the issue has taken place.

7.5 WHO WILL BE THE NOMINATED ADVISERS?

The qualifications for nominated advisers are discussed below (see **7.6**). They are such that brokers, lawyers and accountants will be eligible as will banks and merchant banks and other corporate finance houses. The eligibility criteria are such that they must be established organisations rather than individuals.

It appears unlikely that the merchant banks will become involved in AIM, at least in the early days. They appear to want to see how the market develops. Their cost structures are likely to make the lower fees that can be earned from smaller companies less attractive to them, though they could become more interested if they see AIM developing as an alternative to the Official List rather than a feeder market. In that case, AIM may become the home of larger companies. There are, for comparison, six USM companies capitalised at more than £100m. Invariably the merchant banks we have spoken to would want to carry out the same procedures for AIM as they would for the Official List, reducing many of the cost advantages of the new market.

While the broking arms of the clearing banks are looking at actively sponsoring new issues and marketing AIM and Official List securities to their clients, they are not yet sufficiently organised to be able to perform the role of nominated broker or of nominated adviser. Their corporate finance skills are located within their merchant banking arms and personnel would need to be recruited or transferred and systems would have to be established. However, we believe that the clearing banks will be performing these roles by the end of the decade.

The smaller corporate finance houses that have been active in BES schemes will be keen to be involved in AIM and may wish to make use of their extensive mailing lists to attract new investors. It is not clear how many will be able to meet the size and experience requirements published by the Exchange.

Although solicitors are able to become sponsors to companies joining the Official List we are not aware of any that have done so. Similarly, we can see little attraction to them performing this role for AIM.

There are general qualifications that the Exchange may, at its discretion, impose on nominated advisers that are additional to the detailed ones specified in **7.6** below. They relate to the independence of the nominated adviser and there are therefore particular issues that arise with regard to accountants who may carry out other work for an issuer.

7.5.1 Independence of the nominated adviser

Because of the important role played by the nominated adviser, it must be completely independent of the issuer. The nominated adviser should neither control nor be controlled by the issuer (30% of the voting rights is the guideline for control). In order to be independent it would seem that the adviser should also have no material interest in the success of a flotation. This would appear to preclude the remuneration of the nominated adviser depending upon the success of the flotation.

Accountants

While the nominated adviser may be the auditor, they should not be the reporting accountants. This is at variance with the practice for the Official List, where it is possible for an accountancy firm to be both sponsor and reporting accountant. It therefore reflects the importance placed by the Exchange on the independence of the role and greater continuing duties of the nominated adviser.

The qualifications published by the Exchange for registering as a nominated adviser (see **7.6** below) will be hard for smaller firms of accountants to meet and will probably restrict the role to 'top 20' accountants. However, since a nominated adviser cannot be the reporting accountant, the accountancy firms may be reluctant to hand this role to a competitor, since that might lead to a loss of audit or other advisory work. Accountancy firms may, therefore, not be particularly keen to build a role as nominated advisers, unless they can persuade the Exchange to change this rule. On the other hand, some auditors may be content to cover this through a 'no-poaching' agreement. Reporting accountants will not be necessary where a company is not raising new funds and accountants may be more interested in being nominated advisers. However, if a firm of accountants wishes to be both auditor and nominated adviser then the Exchange will need to be convinced that there is a clear separation of the roles, with different partners in different departments performing them and effective 'Chinese Walls' between them.

For smaller transactions there is likely to be pressure from brokers to perform both roles, arguing that they can perform the dual role more cheaply than two separate firms can. The broker is central to finding the investors for a new issue, has the skills to perform the advisory role too and will therefore be keen to gain the fee from it also. In addition, since the brokers lend their name to an issue they will want to be sure it is they who control the risks to their reputation. They can best achieve this by being the nominated adviser as well. There may be some difference of approach between brokers of different size, eg:

- large brokers may not be very interested in getting involved in detailed documentation issues and will be happy to work with accountants;
- medium sized brokers may be keen to have the adviser's fees as well as the broking fees;
- small brokers may not have sufficient staff to qualify as nominated advisers.

We believe the outcome is likely to go the way of the broker/adviser much of the time. Similarly, smaller firms of brokers may establish informal links with accountants or lawyers to offer a service that appears, to the client, as if it is provided by a combined firm.

7.6 QUALIFICATIONS TO BE A NOMINATED ADVISER

Applicants to be registered as nominated advisers must apply formally to the Exchange on Form NA1 and their executives must apply on Form NA2 (see Appendices 1 and 2 respectively). Their qualifications are open to some discretion from the Exchange and there is provision for work experience to be taken into account instead of formal qualifications. Broadly the requirements are as follows:

1 *Depth*: the adviser must have at least four 'suitably qualified and experienced staff'.
2 *Experience*: the firm must have been acting in a 'principal corporate advisory role for at least three years'. At least four of the executive staff must have been involved in at least three transactions where the firm has acted in a principal corporate advisory role over this three-year period.
3 *Qualifications*: the firm's executive staff must either have passed the relevant examinations of the Securities and Futures Authority or the Exchange or they must have been granted exemption as a result of experience gained under supervision.
4 *Regulation*: the firm must either be a member firm of the Exchange or a member of one of the Self Regulating Organisations authorised under the Financial Services Act 1986.
5 *Supervision*: the Exchange must be satisfied that the applicant firm has satisfactory supervision and control procedures.

The application to be a nominated adviser must be accompanied by a, non-returnable, £1,000 fee and thereafter the cost is £500 per annum. The Exchange will want to be satisfied that the firm is well established and reputable.

7.7 DUTIES OF NOMINATED BROKER

A nominated broker must be a member firm of the London Stock Exchange.

The nominated broker is required to promote trading in the shares of the issuer by (Rule 17.4):

1 *Matching bargains*: the broker should use best endeavours to find a matching buyer for a seller (or vice versa), if there is no market maker in the securities. This duty only applies during normal trading hours, known as the mandatory quote period.

Brokers will become known for dealing in certain stocks, where they are nominated brokers, or perhaps for specialist sectors. As a result they will be approached by buyers or sellers and be able to match bargains. Matching bargains may take several days or even several weeks, depending upon the size of the buy or sell order. This is not the instant dealing achieved through a market maker but it must be remembered that even on the Official List large buy and sell orders for smaller companies may effectively be matched bargains.

2 *Provision of information to the market*: the nominated broker will be required to input, and regularly update, information through the Stock Exchange Alternative Trading Service (SEATS PLUS).

The information currently indicated is:

- number of shares in issue
- percentage of shares in public hands
- turnover
- profit (before and after tax)
- date of announcement of annual and interim results
- dividend

but the Exchange is at liberty to extend this requirement as it sees fit.

3 *Either the nominated broker or the nominated adviser may agree to take on additional duties such as*:

- acting as an intermediary and point of contact with investors
- producing brokers' reports on the company
- generating investor interest in the company
- advising the company on investor's sentiment.

Discussions with potential institutional investors make it clear that the production of brokers' reports, probably by the nominated broker, will be very important in creating and maintaining interest in the market. Companies who wish to see a good aftermarket in their shares would be wise to ensure that this is part of the agreement with their brokers.

7.8 MARKET MAKER

There are at least four firms that, at the time of writing, have indicated they intend to be market makers in AIM shares: J P Jenkins, Winterflood Securities (UBS) and Collins Stewart. Jenkins has been active in making markets in Rule 4.2 companies while Winterflood has been the main market maker for USM companies. These two seem likely to make markets in the majority of AIM stocks. Collins Stewart is both a broker and also makes markets in a number of securities traded under Rule 4.2 and seems likely to make markets on a selective basis in perhaps a dozen stocks. Others are considering being market makers but seem likely to wait to see how the market develops in the first 6 to 12 months.

The market maker generally has no direct relationship with the company but earns its living by the spread between its bid and offer prices. However there have, apparently, been instances of market makers seeking a retainer as an inducement to quoting firm prices. The main AIM market makers have indicated that they do not propose to do this, at the outset at least. Brokers bringing a company to the market may also wish to act as a market maker in their securities. Clearly, the more market makers who are available to trade in a security, the more active the trading will be and competition may have a beneficial effect on the market price and the spread.

For a market maker to trade in a company's securities they want there to be sufficient shares in free float and trading activity in them to make a worthwhile market. Free float refers to the shares in issue that are not owned by directors, employees and connected persons. It is not a tightly defined term because it is a matter of judgement whether the shares of a substantial shareholder are 'free' or not. The market maker wants there to be a large value of shares, with as many as possible in free float and held by a large number of different shareholders. A company with small capitalisation and, say, only 10% of its shares in free float, probably all held by a handful of investors, is unlikely to find a market maker for its shares.

A market maker must be registered in a security with the Exchange in order to trade in it. If it ceases to make a market in that security then it must wait at least three months before reregistering. This will prevent the market maker responding to short-term trading conditions by dropping and restarting trading in a security which might lead to uncertainty and instability in the market.

During the mandatory quote period, a registered market maker must display on SEAQ one of three types of price:

- firm continuous two-way prices; or
- indicative continuous two-way prices; or
- indicative continuous mid-prices.

These prices must be in, at least, the minimum quote size in each security in which it is registered. It will be clear from the SEAQ screen whether the price is firm or indicative.

The minimum quote size will generally be 500 shares, set by the Exchange. There is a formula for calculating the 'normal market size', which is described in the Glossary. This will not be relevant for most AIM securities since the calculation is likely to put them into the lowest band. Nonetheless this does not prevent a market maker from quoting for bigger sizes; it is quite common for a market maker to quote a firm price for 1,000 or 2,000 shares although the minimum size demanded by the Exchange would be 500.

If one market maker is quoting firm prices then all who are registered in the security must do so. If firm prices are quoted then the market maker must deal with any member firm at that price in share quantities up to the size for which the price is quoted. If indicative prices are quoted then the market maker must quote a firm price on enquiry over the telephone. If the systems of the Exchange or market maker are unable to cope with the volume of transactions then a 'fast market' may be declared and the market maker registered in a security will not be obliged to deal at the displayed price but must still quote a firm price over the telephone.

The market maker must close its quotation within 15 minutes of the end of the mandatory quote period and must not alter its quotation in the meantime.

CHAPTER 8

Public announcements

8.1 INTRODUCTION

One of the guiding principles of AIM is that information should be disclosed to enable investors to make informed judgements. This particularly relates to the Admission Document, which will not be vetted by the Exchange before it is sent to potential investors. There will also be continuing responsibilities on issuers to disclose information. Such public disclosure through announcements will generally take the place of expensive shareholder circulars. This will be far less costly than the circulars required by the rules of the Official List which may contain accountants' reports, experts' reports, working capital and indebtedness statements. It should also enable transactions to be completed more quickly, without the need for shareholder approval at a general meeting.

Disclosure will be achieved by sending an announcement to the Company Announcements Office of the Stock Exchange which will then release the information on its electronic information network (Regulatory News Service RNS) and will place this on display at its premises. A wide range of banks, brokers, institutional investors etc take the RNS through data providers and announcements are picked up by the press agencies. An A, in blue, goes on the relevant security page on SEATS to inform dealers that there has been a company announcement. The regulations actually refer to 'notification to the Company Announcements Office' but this has the same meaning as making an announcement, since the Office will relay the text through its information systems. The notification must be in English and in writing.

Six copies of the announcement are required, although it is common to send an initial electronic message which is then followed by the documents. This requirement for six copies extends to all documents sent to shareholders eg circulars, report and accounts. These copies of communications to shareholders need only be sent to the Exchange at the time they are sent to shareholders.

The RNS ensures:

- security – a password system is used to confirm that messages received are authentic;
- dissemination.

That information is then rapidly distributed to the whole market.

The issuer or its agent can send information as word processed text through the Direct Input Provider (DIP) service which uses a dial up facility to the Exchange. Larger companies may have their own direct link but we would expect AIM companies to use an agent who may be their broker, a financial public relations company or a registrar service. The facility is set up through application to the Company Announcements Office (CAO).

The full text of the announcement is checked and retransmitted to information resellers through a digital feed. The DIP facility can receive announcements 24 hours per day, 7 days per week throughout the year. The target time from receipt to release of messages is 15 minutes (during the hours given below) and includes validation and authorisation of release. Announcements are distributed from 7.30 am to 6.00 pm Monday to Friday (excluding Bank Holidays).

Responsibility remains firmly with the issuer for the accuracy of the information published through the Exchange and for it not being defamatory. The Exchange may require a change to text or an indemnity in respect of an announcement that may be defamatory. There is a copyback facility available for users of DIP to check that the text received by the Exchange is the same as that sent by the issuer. The CAO may decline to publish information that is not required for compliance with the Regulations of AIM since the service is not intended for other publicity purposes.

The announcements must also be available free of charge to the public at an address in the UK. The address must be stated in the announcement and the documents must be available for 14 days. This permits people who have heard about an announcement and want to see its full text to get hold of it.

8.2 PRICE SENSITIVE INFORMATION

The Company Announcements Office of the Stock Exchange must be notified of information that is not public knowledge, which falls into the classes (a) and (b) listed below and which is likely to lead to a substantial movement in the price of listed securities.

(a) *Developments*

An issuer is required to make an announcement if there are major new developments in a company's 'sphere of activity' which may lead to a substantial change in the price of its securities. This is further broadened to relate to the company's assets, liabilities, financial position or the general course of its business. This last consideration is probably the most important, covering future trading prospects. An example of this would be a pharmaceutical company which is developing a new drug, which it has told investors about, and has been refused certification or has conducted a disappointing trial. Since the original information about the potential for the product is known and its implications are included in the share price, the setback must be announced if there is likely to be a substantial effect on the share price.

This requirement relates also to traded debt securities to the extent that the news may lead to a substantial movement in their price. There is an added requirement for disclosure relating to debt securities if the news may 'significantly affect its ability to meet its commitments' (Rule 16.14.b). Since this would also affect the price of its securities it is not clear that this adds to the responsibilities of the issuer. It possibly gives some clarification.

(b) *Changes*

An issuer is required to make an announcement if there is a change in its financial condition or prospects and if knowledge of this change is likely to lead to a substantial change in the price of its traded securities.

This provision would cover trading results that were much poorer or much better than market expectations.

8.2.1 Priority of disclosure

The Company Announcements Office must be notified, without delay, and before the information is given to anyone else and this includes announcement at a meeting of shareholders. The procedure is to time the lodging of an announcement with the Company Announcements Office so that it will be put out through the dealing screen system just before the shareholders meeting is given the information. This ensures that investors 'in the market' are not disadvantaged. It might be argued that all those who are not at dealing screens or close to a telephone will be disadvantaged but this system seems to be the least unfair one available.

There are two exemptions to this rule demanding first notification to the Exchange: advisers and regulatory authorities (see **8.2.3** below) may be given information either before an announcement is made or if no announcement is made.

8.2.2 Exemptions

An issuer need not make an announcement about impending developments or matters that are being negotiated. Because these matters are uncertain a premature announcement would be misleading, so there is time for them to become clear (Rule 16.16).

However, there may be instances when confidential information is shared, for example with advisers, and the issuer becomes aware that a breach of confidence has occurred or 'is likely to occur'. In these cases an announcement must be made. If the matters are still so uncertain that there is little that can be said, there is provision to make a warning announcement that the issuer expects to make a fuller announcement shortly.

If an issuer considers that public disclosure of information might prejudice its interests then it may apply to the Exchange for a dispensation to excuse it from the rules. An example might be a commercial arrangement which, if announced, would alert competitors and allow them to prepare. One could foresee a short period being permitted to complete negotiations despite rumours circulating in the market.

8.2.3 Sharing confidential information

The issuer may give confidential, price sensitive information to certain people in confidence (Rule 16.16.b). Such people must be informed that they cannot deal in the traded securities of the issuer and that they must keep the information confidential. Permitted parties include:

1. *Advisers*: this relates to its own advisers or those of other parties involved in the matter.
2. *Negotiating parties*: this relates to prospective financiers as well as those with whom a negotiation is being done directly.
3. *Employee representatives*: a company may be required to share information with employee representatives or trade unions.
4. *Government*: government and statutory bodies, and regulators such as the Monopolies and Mergers Commission, the Bank of England, DTI or the Gaming Board, are entitled to receive price sensitive information in confidence. Notification to them does not automatically require disclosure through the Company Announcements Office of the Stock Exchange (Rule 16.16.c). The duty to make announcements continues to be covered by the other AIM Rules.

8.2.4 Timing

Information must be disclosed 'without delay'. The key consideration is that information that may influence the company's share price should not become known to some investors before others, giving them an unfair advantage. The longer the delay in releasing information the more likely that it will become known in an uncontrolled manner through rumour or unauthorised disclosure. In practice there is some flexibility to permit the company to clarify the detail and implications of the information before making an announcement. However, if the share price of an issuer changed sharply before it made an announcement, then the Exchange might deem the delay to have been unreasonable on the basis that the facts speak for themselves. The company and its directors might then risk censure.

8.2.5 Materiality

Rule 16.14 states that for an announcement to be necessary the price movement that may occur should be substantial. In the case of uncertainty it is best to err on the side of caution. An issuer would be unable to use the excuse of believing the information would not cause a substantial price movement if events subsequently show that it did.

8.3 DIRECTORS' INTERESTS

The issuer is required to notify the Company Announcements Office of changes in the interests of directors and 'connected persons' in securities that either are or will be traded on AIM. A connected person is defined in s 346 of the Companies Act 1985. It broadly refers to family, friends and business associates (see Glossary). It is intended to ensure that people who have shared interests and who might act in concert are required to disclose the actions any of them may take. This should, for instance, prevent directors from using an undisclosed nominee to trade shares secretly on their behalf.

The information notified must include the following details:

1 The date when disclosure was made to the issuer.
   — The issuer must notify the Exchange without delay once it is informed of the transaction.
2 The date of the transaction.
3 The price, amount and class of securities bought or sold.
4 The nature of the transaction.
   — The nature of the transaction is not just restricted to a sale or purchase but includes also the exercise, purchase or sale of options to buy or sell securities. It would appear also to cover giving a charge over shares to a bank or other person (see **10.1**).
5 The nature and extent of the director's interest in the transaction.
6 The identity of the director and connected person and the nature of the connection between them (if this is relevant).
7 Where a director has been given permission to deal during a closed period due to exceptional circumstances (see Chapter 10) the notification to the Company Announcements Office must include a statement explaining the nature of those exceptional circumstances.

Non-UK companies whose shares may be traded on AIM will not be covered by the Companies Act 1985 and therefore may not have access to the information that the Act requires shareholders to disclose. Nonetheless, such issuers are still required to notify the information, as far as it is known to them.

8.4 SUBSTANTIAL TRANSACTIONS

A substantial transaction is defined in the rules as one where any of the ratios, listed in **8.4.1** below, is 10% or more (Rule 16.23.b). It should include transactions carried out by a subsidiary of an issuer. Where a substantial transaction occurs then a public announcement must be made but AIM carries the great advantage (over the Official List or USM) that a circular to shareholders will seldom be required. Therefore a company will be able to make acquisitions without having to seek shareholder approval save as may be required under company law. More particularly, circulars including reports by independent experts and working capital reports will not be required nor the detailed financial information required of companies on the Official List.

The figures used to calculate whether an announcement is necessary shall be taken from the last published consolidated annual accounts or any contained in a preliminary announcement of annual results. Since some companies make a preliminary announcement of their results some weeks before sending out printed documents, this provision allows a company to use the latest audited figures during this intervening period.

8.4.1 Tests for a substantial transaction

(i) Assets. The net assets acquired or disposed of divided by the net assets of the issuer

The net assets of the issuer are defined as the total of its share capital and reserves, excluding minority interests.

The acquisition or disposal of net assets may make the difference between an entire business being consolidated or not consolidated in future. In such cases it is the net assets of that entire business which should be used in the calculation and not just the assets that are the subject of the transaction. This relates to the purchase or sale of a stake in a company which may change its status from a subsidiary to an associate or vice versa.

For a transaction relating to part or all of an undertaking:

1 When this transaction is an acquisition, net assets means the consideration paid.
2 When this transaction is a disposal, the calculation relates to the value of the net assets included in the last published accounts of the issuer.

Where the transaction does not relate to an undertaking but only to certain assets such as a property or machinery, without the accompanying business, then:

1 For an acquisition, net assets means the greater of book value or the value of consideration paid.
   (a) It is not clear that a vendor will always be obliged to divulge the book value of assets it is selling, so the book value of assets acquired may not be known. In such cases the consideration paid must be the measure used.
2 For a disposal, net assets means their book value in the last published consolidated annual accounts of the issuer.

(ii) Profits. The profits acquired or sold divided by the profits of the issuer

Profits are defined as those after deducting all charges except for taxation and extraordinary items, as used in the preparation of the last published annual consolidated accounts (or preliminary announcement).

The acquisition or disposal of a particular parcel of shares may make the difference between an entire business being consolidated or not consolidated in future. In such cases it is the profits of that entire business which should be used in the calculation and not just those that relate to the transaction.

(iii) Consideration to assets. The consideration paid or received divided by the net assets of the issuer

(iv) Consideration to market capitalisation. The consideration paid or received divided by the aggregate market value of all the equity shares of the issuer

The consideration is the amount paid to the vendors and therefore excludes fees, commissions and expenses (Rule 16.23.i.ii). However, one would expect these to be disclosed under the 'catch-all' requirement (see **8.4.3** 'Effect of the transaction').

Where part or all of the consideration is in the form of securities to be traded on an exchange then the consideration is the market value of those securities. Although the AIM Rule 16.23.i.i refers to securities traded on the London Stock Exchange and does not mention overseas exchanges, it would be hard to justify any valuation other than market value on those exchanges.

Although the rules do not say when a valuation of securities should be done, it would be reasonable to take the price at the last practical moment before the transaction takes place. The price used for valuation should be the bid price of the securities, being the price for which they could be sold.

If there is an element of deferred or conditional consideration then the consideration used in this test is the maximum that could be paid. There is no provision in the rules for discounting payments in the future to reach a present value.

Despite these specific requirements, the Exchange retains the discretion to disregard the calculations and substitute other indicators they believe to be an appropriate indication of the size and materiality of the transaction (Rule 16.23.b). In most cases we would expect directors to want to issue announcements in order to stimulate investor interest, rather than having to be forced to disclose information by these rules.

8.4.2 Exemptions

The following transactions are exempted from the requirement to make an announcement concerning them under AIM Rule 16.22. However, if they are likely to lead to a substantial change in the issuer's share price then they will require an announcement under AIM Rule 16.14 or 16.15 (see **8.2** above).

1 A transaction both of a revenue nature and in the ordinary course of business.
  — It is sometimes not obvious what constitutes the 'ordinary course of business' since this may relate to matters that the particular issuer has not undertaken before. It will apply to transactions that the particular issuer or similar businesses carry out with some regularity and which are directly related to the trade of the company. Therefore the forward purchase of currency may be in the ordinary course of business but the purchase of a substantial piece of equipment would fail the test of being a revenue item.

2 An issue of securities or other transaction to raise finance.
  — This must not involve the purchase or sale of fixed assets. If such a transaction were associated then it would have to be announced.

3 Any transaction by an issuer which does not have equity securities traded on AIM.

8.4.3 Details to be announced

The information that should be clearly stated in the announcement is detailed below.

Details of the transaction

This includes details of any company or business that is involved in the transaction. The rule uses the phrase 'where this is relevant'. It will usually be relevant and there can be few occasions when there is a reason to omit it.

Description of the business

The business that uses the assets that are the subject of the transaction should be described. For example, the acquisition of a new subsidiary would require that the business of that undertaking should be described. If the transaction related to assets that are a part of one or more businesses then those businesses should be described. The intention of this rule is to allow the shareholder to understand what effect the transaction may have on the issuer.

Consideration

The amount paid or received should be detailed as well as 'how it is being satisfied'. Forgiveness of debt, issue of loan notes and cash are all possible methods of settling the consideration and should be disclosed. For example, if a bank loan had been negotiated to pay for a purchase then that should be disclosed. The announcement should also include the terms of any deferred consideration, including conditional payments. The conditions should be clearly stated (Rule 16.22.c).

The rules call for 'the maximum total consideration' to be given (Rule 16.23.i.iii). In some circumstances this may be difficult to know for certain, such as when the consideration is due in a foreign currency at a future and therefore uncertain exchange rate. There may also be occasions when the total consideration may not be limited or capped and could, in theory, be greater than the net worth of the acquiring company. In such cases, legal advice must be taken and the Exchange may need to be consulted because there is a risk that the transaction might be classed as a reverse takeover.

Where all or part of the consideration is paid in the form of securities traded on the Official List, USM or AIM then the mid-market price should be used for valuation. The valuation date is not specified in the rules but should be that used for valuation in the transaction contract itself; if there is no such applicable date then the closest practical date to the announcement date should be taken.

While the rules make no specific reference to securities traded on other stock exchanges, issuers are expected to use common sense and would normally be expected to apply similar valuation criteria to such securities.

Value of assets

The value of net assets included in the transaction should be stated. This should be the greater of the consideration or book value.

There may be occasions when the book value of assets acquired may not be revealed by the vendor or where the book value is at an unreasonable level. In such instances the issuer should seek guidance from the Exchange which will look at all the circumstances on a case-by-case basis.

Profits attributable to the transaction

It is the profits 'attributable' to the net assets acquired or disposed of that should be announced. The meaning of attributable may be difficult to define and open to some interpretation. In the case of a sale, it would relate to the increase in profitability resulting from the transaction. In the case of a purchase, the term cannot refer to uncertain future profits but only to demonstrable past profits associated with those assets or certain changes their acquisition will have on future profits.

Effect on the issuer

The effect of the transaction on the issuer appears to be covered by the points above. However, the rules add this extra 'catch-all' requirement that the issuer must explain the effects the transaction may have on it, if there is anything that is not covered by these previous requirements. The issuer should be careful to avoid saying anything that could be construed as a profit forecast since this might require an accountant's report in the case of a future bid for the company.

Directors' service contracts

If the transaction involves the appointment of new directors then details of their service contracts must be included in the announcement.

Application of sale proceeds

How the proceeds are to be spent must be announced also. The information released is often limited to 'reduction in group borrowings' but some companies choose to be more explicit and make statements such as 'will be available for future acquisition opportunities'.

A related issue is how the issuer will deal with securities such as shares or loan notes received as consideration for a sale. The issuer must announce its intention to hold or sell such securities.

Effect of the transaction

The purpose of all these specific requirements is to enable investors to understand and evaluate the effect a transaction will have on the issuer and on their investment. The final 'catch-all' clause (Rule 16.22.j) requires the issuer to announce any other information that is necessary to enable investors to evaluate these effects. If the issuer were to hold back information that is not specifically required but which subsequently proves to have been relevant, then there is a danger of incurring sanctions (see Chapter 12).

8.5 TRANSACTION WITH A RELATED PARTY

The purpose of these provisions is to prevent directors from doing deals on favourable terms with themselves or their families, to the disadvantage of shareholders. The control is that such dealings must be notified to shareholders if they are substantial and who may bring the matter before a general meeting or can seek redress through the courts. There is no requirement under the AIM Rules for such transactions to be approved by shareholders; however this is demanded by s 320 of the Companies Act 1985 and the notice convening the extraordinary general meeting must contain all the information that may be necessary to make a properly informed decision. The result is that the amount of information that will need to be gathered, verified and disclosed will be less, with an accompanying reduction in cost of the transaction. Specifically, there would be no requirement for an independent adviser to have advised the directors that the transaction is fair and reasonable, nor for an independent valuation of assets nor for a working capital nor an indebtedness statement. It may be considered best practice that a company engaged in a transaction with a related party should publish some of this information. For example, it may seek an independent valuation and investor confidence might be significantly affected if it failed to do that. Nonetheless, costs of compliance ought to be significantly less than on the Official List.

A transaction with a related party must be notified to the Company Announcements Office if any of the ratios relating to substantial transactions and listed in **8.4.1** exceeds 5% (Rule 16.24). The details announced must be as for a substantial transaction, described in **8.4.3** (Rule 16.22), and include the name of the related party and the details of the 'nature and extent' of that party's interest in the transaction.

The issuer must send a copy of the announcement to its shareholders at least seven days prior to the transaction being entered into. As described elsewhere, the Exchange must be notified before shareholders.

Whether or not an announcement is required, if any of the ratios described in **8.4.1** (Rule 16.23) exceeds 0.25% then details must be included in the next published annual accounts of the company. The details must include the identity of the related party, the value of the consideration and all other relevant circumstances. The term relevant circumstances is not defined in the AIM Rules but should be interpreted widely rather than narrowly. As with other matters which are not defined, a subsequent challenge might result in the Exchange applying sanctions against an individual or a company as described in Chapter 12.

8.5.1 Definition of related party

A related party is a director of the issuer, a substantial shareholder in it or an associate of a person covered by the following definitions.

A director

This refers to a director of the issuer at the time of the transaction. The term includes a director of a parent company or of a subsidiary or of a fellow subsidiary of a common parent. It also covers someone who held such a position within the 12 months preceding the transaction. It also covers a shadow director. A shadow director is someone whose instructions the employees of the business customarily follow. Therefore someone who acts and is obeyed as a director is treated as one regardless of their strict legal position.

Any substantial shareholder

A substantial shareholder is someone who is entitled to vote or control the votes of 10% or more of the votes at a general meeting.

An associate

This relates to an associate of a director or a substantial shareholder, as described above. It would normally be quite clear who is an associate but the term is defined carefully in an attempt to close all possible loopholes. It relates to the following:

1 An individual's spouse or child.

2 Trustees of a trust of which the individual or their family is a beneficiary or may be a beneficiary (as would occur in a discretionary trust).

 This is complicated by an exemption for an occupational pension scheme or for an employee share scheme. In turn, this exemption is restricted if these special types of trust confer benefits on individuals who are all (or most of whom are) related parties. A transaction with a director's personal pension scheme, or a pension scheme whose membership was restricted to directors, would therefore be deemed as being with a related party.

3 Any company in which persons defined as a 'director' or 'substantial shareholder' (see above) or members of their family have an interest and are able to:

- exercise 30% of the votes at general meetings; or
- appoint or remove directors holding a majority of voting rights at board meetings.

 The interest may be actual or potential, so that if a child of a director of an issuer had an option to acquire shares in a company which, in turn acquired assets from the issuer, then this would be a transaction with a related person.

This section also applies to a company where joint related parties can exercise this control. This means that there must be disclosure if a director or substantial shareholder act together with other parties to control a company and that undertakes a transaction with the issuer.

4 Any other company that is a parent, subsidiary or fellow subsidiary of a common parent.

5 Any company of which persons defined as a 'director' or 'substantial shareholder' (see above) is a shadow director.

8.6 OTHER ANNOUNCEMENTS REQUIRED

The issuer is also required to make announcements in a number of other areas (see paras **8.6.1–8.6.5** below).

8.6.1 Significant shareholdings

Sections 198 to 208 of the Companies Act 1985 require that a shareholder or group of people acting in concert must notify a company once they have a stake of 3% or more in the equity of a company. Further they must, once this threshold has been reached, inform the company of transactions in its shares that meet the following criteria:

- recross the threshold;
- fractional percentage shareholdings are rounded to the nearest whole number below. It is necessary to inform the company of changes of 1% on this basis.

The company must be informed of relevant transactions within five days. This requirement is extended by the City Code on Takeovers and Mergers which requires notification both to the company and to the Stock Exchange for 1% movements above 15% of the voting rights in a company. These must be notified by 12 noon on the day following a transaction.

Under s 212 of the Companies Act a company is permitted to demand details of the beneficial ownership of shares. This power enables it to discover disguised shareholders who may, for instance, be seeking to build up a substantial stake with a view to making a bid for the company. The s 212 procedure gives another weapon to company management to discover what is happening. If a shareholder does not respond, within a reasonable time, to the demand for the identity of the beneficial owner of shares then the company has powers to disenfranchise those shares and to prevent their transfer to anyone else.

The issuer must announce any shareholdings of 3% or more and transactions by such substantial shareholders that are either notified to it or which it discovers under s 212 procedures. The announcement must include:

- the identity of the shareholder and connected parties;
- the percentage holding;
- the date on which the issuer was informed of the shareholding;
- the date the transaction was effected.

Non-UK companies whose shares may be traded on AIM will not be covered by the Companies Act 1985 and therefore may not have access to the information that the Act requires shareholders to disclose. Nonetheless, such issuers are still required to notify the information, as far as it is known to them.

8.6.2 Changes in directors

The resignation, removal or appointment of directors must be announced through the Exchange. The announcement must include the same information about new directors as required in the Admission Document, namely:

1 Their directorships over the previous five years.
2 Any unspent convictions.
3 Details of personal bankruptcies.
4 Receiverships or liquidations.
   — This applies to companies where the director of the issuer was a director at the time of the event or within the 12 months before it.
5 Any public criticisms by statutory or regulatory authorities.
   — This would refer to published reports of DTI investigators, as well as reports by liquidators or receivers. It would also include censure by the Stock Exchange or professional bodies of which the director was a member.

8.6.3 Issue or cancellation of securities

The issuer must notify the Company Announcements Office if it issues new securities, whether of an existing or new class and whether or not traded on AIM. Similarly, it must notify the CAO regarding the cancellation of securities that are traded on AIM.

8.6.4 Information on dividends

This requirement includes all distributions, including dividends, capital distribution or interest payment on AIM securities. An announcement must be made of any decision to pay or withhold a distribution. Details must be given of:

1. *The net amount payable*: the text uses the word 'exact amount' which means that rounding is not acceptable.
2. *The payment date*: this is the date on which cheques are dated and sent out.
3. *The record date*: where this is applicable it is the date or period to which the payment relates.
4. *Tax information*: any foreign income dividend election and any income tax treated as paid at the lower rate and not repayable.

8.6.5 Publication of accounts

The Company Announcements Office must be informed of the publication of annual audited accounts. This duty must be carried out without delay, suggesting that they should be told no later than the day they are sent to shareholders.

8.7 AGGREGATION OF TRANSACTIONS

Aggregation is used to prevent a series of connected transactions escaping the rules which require issuers to make announcements in certain situations. Without these provisions, a series of acquisitions or disposals could be arranged so that each was below the threshold requiring announcement yet, after they were all completed, the company could have been transformed.

Transactions that have been completed since the date of the last published audited balance sheet must be taken together with the latest transaction in order to apply the thresholds listed above and in Chapter 9. However, if an Admission Document has been issued since the last audited balance sheet then the relevant date is the date of that document. The aggregation rules apply in the following circumstances:

1 *Same party*: if the transactions are entered into with the same party or with connected parties (see **8.3**).
2 *Same company*: if the transactions all relate to dealings in the securities of (or an interest in) the same company.
3 *New business activity*: if, taken together, they lead to a substantial involvement in a new business activity which was not previously a part of the issuer's principal business activities.

This final requirement is a matter of judgement on a number of counts; it may not be clear what previously was, or was not, a principal activity nor what constitutes a substantial involvement. It may not even always be clear what constitutes a new business activity; for instance a construction company might argue that a venture into house building was essentially the same business although specialist house builders might disagree.

CHAPTER 9

Automatic suspension of trading

9.1 REVERSE TAKEOVERS

The Exchange will automatically suspend trading in securities of a company that is the subject of a reverse takeover. A reverse takeover is defined as an acquisition or a series of acquisitions in a 12-month period which either:

- causes the ratios described in **10.3** above to exceed 100%; or
- leads to a fundamental change in the nature of the business; or
- leads to a change in board or voting control of the issuer.

In such circumstances, the issuer must send an explanatory circular to shareholders and seek approval from them prior to the reverse takeover proceeding.

9.1.1 Explanatory circular

The content of the circular is not described in the AIM Rules but it must clearly be such as to provide a clear explanation and justification to shareholders. Unlike the Rules of the Official List there is no requirement to obtain approval from the Exchange before sending a circular. We believe that if the nature of the company has completely changed as a result of such transactions best practice would be to follow the Official List requirements for a Super Class One Circular.

In relation to all circulars, the Rules of the Official List require that the explanation they provide should be clear and adequate and contain all the information necessary for shareholders to make an informed decision. In addition, they should carry a heading drawing attention to the importance of the document and recommending that investors who are doubtful of what action to take should consult appropriate advisers.

A Super Class One Circular for an Official List company includes (London Stock Exchange Listing Rules Chapter 10):

- details of the transaction;
- a description of any business involved;
- the consideration, how it is to be satisfied, details of deferred consideration;
- the value of net assets subject to the transaction;
- profits attributable to net assets acquired;
- the expected effects of the transaction on the AIM company;
- a statement on the group's prospects;
- an accountant's report on any profit forecast;
- details of service contracts of proposed directors;
- directors' interests in shares, transactions and details of their service contracts;
- a comparative table, setting out in similar format three years' accounts of the issuer and the acquired business, including
  - profit & loss account
  - balance sheet
  - cash flow statement
  - accounting policies
  - notes covering at least the last two balance sheets and all three profit & loss accounts and cash flow statements

  (in certain circumstances where a comparative table is not appropriate an accountant's report would be required);
- a statement from directors that the enlarged enterprise has sufficient working capital for its requirements;
- a statement of indebtedness;
- details of litigation;
- material changes since last accounts;
- major interests in the shares of the company.

Clearly, AIM companies may seek to take advantage of the fact that the Rules for the AIM market do not demand reports by accountants or experts. It will be for the directors and their nominated advisers to judge what their investors will want.

9.1.2 Seek approval from shareholders prior to the transaction proceeding

A general meeting must be called to give approval by a simple majority of the votes cast. Any agreement on a transaction must therefore be conditional on shareholder approval. If it is the final transaction of a series that results in automatic suspension then it will be this that requires a circular and shareholder approval.

If shareholder approval is given then the Exchange will discontinue the admission of the securities to AIM. The issuer will have to reapply for admission to AIM and will have to submit a new Admission Document.

If shareholder approval is not given or if the transaction is not completed then the suspension will be lifted – unless there are other relevant circumstances, such as the resignation of the nominated adviser or nominated broker.

CHAPTER 10

Model Code for share dealing

The following paragraphs describe limits on the ability of directors to deal in the securities of a company where they are a director. The same constraints apply to 'relevant employees'. A relevant employee is one who is employed by the issuer, its parent or subsidiary and who is likely to have unpublished price sensitive information. In the following sections, therefore, the term director includes relevant employees.

10.1 DEFINITION OF DEALING

The definition of dealing for the purpose of the Model Code contains a number of inclusions and exclusions, as discussed below.

10.1.1 Inclusions

The meaning of the term 'dealing' is wider than just the sale or purchase of securities. It also covers an agreement to buy or sell securities as well as dealing in options (to buy or sell) on securities.

Dealing transactions are interpreted very strictly and include;

1 Bed and breakfast: the sale of securities before the end of a tax year, followed by their repurchase at the beginning of the following tax year is termed a bed and breakfast transaction. It is used to crystallise a profit or loss for the purposes of tax planning.

2 Transfers into Personal Equity Plans.
3 Gifts: the gift of shares to a relative or a charity would count as share dealing and be prohibited under the circumstances outlined here.
4 Transactions between directors: merely because individuals are covered by the Model Code and may possess the same unpublished price sensitive information does not remove the restriction from dealing under the circumstances outlined in that Code.

10.1.2 Exclusions

Dealings, for the purpose of the Model Code, do not include:

1 Personal Equity Plans (PEPs) under certain circumstances.
   However, this will not be material for directors of AIM companies since AIM securities are not eligible for inclusion in a PEP (see **16.2.4**).
2 Savings schemes if:
   (a) they are options under save as you earn (SAYE) or similar schemes; or
   (b) they are effected through regular payment by standing order or direct debit; or
   (c) they relate to a regular mandated reinvestment of dividends or other distributions by the issuer; and
   (d) the restrictions set out for PEPs (see above) are observed.
3 Discretionary investments:
   — dealings by a fund manager of a PEP, unit trust, investment trust etc are excluded as are dealings by the director in those funds.
4 Entitlements as a result of rights issues, scrip issues etc:
   — these include the sale of a part of an entitlement in order to take up the balance.
5 Acceptance of a takeover offer.
6 Transactions with connected persons etc whose interests are treated as those of the director (Companies Act ss 324 and 328).

10.2 RESTRICTIONS ON DEALING

The following paragraphs (**10.2.1–10.2.3**) look at restrictions on the ability of directors to deal in the securities of their companies.

10.2.1 Short-term considerations

A director of an issuer must not deal in its securities 'on considerations [that are] of a short-term nature'. They should not, therefore, sell shares because they believe that share prices generally will drop, only to buy them back a few weeks later when they feel the situation has changed and that share prices will rise.

10.2.2 Close period

A director must not deal in shares during a close period.

A close period is:

1 The two months immediately preceding the preliminary announcement of the company's annual results. If there is less than two months between the end of the financial year and the preliminary announcement then this is the close period.

   There is no obligation on a company to make a preliminary announcement. If it does not do so then the date when results are published would be substituted (note that this eventuality is not explicitly covered in the Model Code). The close period would be the two months prior to publication or, if shorter, the period between the financial year-end and publication.

2 The two months immediately preceding the announcement of half year results (or if there is less than two months between the end of the financial period and the announcement then that shorter period is the close period).

3 The period of one month immediately preceding the announcement of the first three quarterly results of the year. The rule for the period before the final results reverts to two months as in point (1) above. Again, if there is less than one month between the end of the financial period and the announcement then this shorter period becomes the close period.

10.2.3 Other restrictions on dealing

A director must not deal in securities of an AIM company when as a director they:

1 Have unpublished price sensitive information: it could be argued that a director always has unpublished price sensitive information, so the restriction demands some common sense. If the director is aware of a change in trading or prospects or is aware of a possible transaction which would be likely to affect the share price substantially then it would be wrong to deal.
2 Do not have written confirmation of clearance to deal: see **10.5** below.

10.3 CLEARANCE TO DEAL

A director must not, in any circumstances, deal in securities of their company without receiving clearance to deal. The application must be recorded as outlined in **10.5** below. This clearance may be given by the chairman or one or more other directors designated by the board for this purpose.

If the chairman or a designated director seek clearance to deal then they must receive clearance to deal from either the board at a board meeting or another designated director.

10.3.1 Ordinary circumstances

This clearance is required for all circumstances. Even outside restricted periods or times when special considerations apply, the directors must get express clearance to deal.

Clearance should not be given:

- during a close period;
- where it is believed that the proposed dealing is of a speculative nature, eg taking advantage of short-term share price movements;
- whenever it is believed that the director may have unpublished price sensitive information.

10.3.2 Exceptional circumstances

Clearance to deal may be given in respect of the exercise of an option under an employee share scheme or in respect of a convertible security even if this occurs during a prohibited period. However, this exception is only permitted if the option could not 'reasonably have been expected' to be exercised earlier and if the right will lapse if not exercised.

The securities acquired under this exception may not, however, be sold during the prohibited period.

10.4 DEALINGS BY CONNECTED PERSONS

A director must try to stop persons connected to him from dealing in securities in his company if they are traded on AIM:

- during a close period;
- during a period when the director has unpublished price sensitive information and would be prohibited from dealing (see **10.3** above).

For this purpose a connected person includes an investment manager acting on behalf of the director or on behalf of another connected person.

This duty can only be carried out as far as it is consistent with a duty of confidentiality. If the director cannot prevent a connected person from dealing without revealing information that should not be disclosed then their first duty is one of confidentiality. While it is not covered by the Code, the director would be wise to notify the board of the problem, in an appropriate manner.

In any case, the director should inform any connected persons or investment managers:

- of the company or companies whose shares are traded on AIM and of which they are a director;
- of the close periods for each company;
- of any other periods when dealing is prohibited (limited by the duty of confidentiality);
- that the director should be advised immediately following dealings in the securities of the issuer traded on AIM.

10.5 RECORD OF DEALINGS

A written record must be maintained of clearances to deal sought and whether clearance was given or refused. Written confirmation must be given to the director concerned. This recording role might be delegated to company secretarial or other appropriate staff but one would expect there to be appropriate control by the board.

A record should be kept of actual dealing in the securities of the issuer by directors, relevant employees, connected persons and investment managers. A list of such dealings should be circulated to directors before board meetings together with the other board papers.

See also **10.3.1** above.

CHAPTER 11

The law on insider dealing

11.1 GENERAL BACKGROUND

The UK law on insider dealing (The Insider Dealing Act) implements the EC directive of 1989 and is contained in Part V of the Criminal Justice Act 1993. Its breach is therefore a criminal offence.

There are also two offences of 'market manipulation' and 'dishonest concealment' under s 47 of the Financial Services Act 1986. Dishonest concealment, for example, would cover cases where an insider sells securities in a company knowing, but concealing, some significant fact about it that would undermine the price of the securities if it were divulged.

By obtaining a trading facility on AIM the directors of a company, its employees, advisers and other individuals, who may have access to unpublished price sensitive information, come under the Insider Dealing Act when dealing in its securities or when giving information about it.

It is an offence for an individual who has information as an insider to deal on a regulated market or either through or as a professional intermediary in securities whose price would be significantly affected if the inside information were made public. It is also an offence to encourage insider dealing and to disclose inside information.

The punishment on conviction is up to seven years' imprisonment and an unlimited fine.

AIM is classified as a regulated market for the purposes of this legislation. We define and explain below some of the more detailed issues relating to insider dealing.

11.2 SCOPE OF DEALING

Dealing includes telling others to deal and can even cover cases where an investment adviser acts without consulting the director or where the director does not benefit.

11.3 DEFINITION OF INSIDER

An insider is someone who:

- is a director, employee or shareholder of an issuer; or
- has access to the inside information by virtue of their employment, office or profession;
- it is also anyone given inside information by an insider.

An individual is not just an insider with respect to their own company but also regarding other companies whose shares trade on AIM or other stock exchanges in the European Community. For example, if you know your company is about to launch a world beating product then you may not sell shares in competitors. This is because you have inside information that their share price is likely to decline significantly.

11.4 PRICE SENSITIVE INFORMATION

Neither the Act nor the Stock Exchange have defined when information is price sensitive. It seems that it falls within this definition if, after it is released, the price of the security changes. It is therefore only with hindsight that one can know whether an offence may be committed. Fortunately, common sense should give sufficient guidance in most cases.

11.5 SIGNIFICANT EFFECT ON PRICE

There is no definition of what is meant by significant in this context. It is felt that a 5% price movement is probably significant but it will depend on the circumstances of the case. A 2% movement in Marks & Spencer's share price would be significant in the context of buying a million shares while a 5% movement might not be in the context of selling a few shares in a very illiquid stock.

11.6 PUBLIC INFORMATION

Information that is public is not covered by this legislation, however it is not always certain when this is the case.

11.6.1 Clear cases

Information will be treated as having been made public when:

1. *It is published in accordance with the rules of a regulated market*: this may be a different market from the one on which the transaction took place.
2. *It is contained in public records*: this may include share registers, data published by government regulatory bodies etc.
3. *It can be readily acquired by those likely to deal in the securities*: this might include asking the company or asking planning authorities for details of permissions sought and granted.
4. *It is derived from other information that has been made public*: this might cover calculations made by analysts or others which they have carried out on information published in company accounts, perhaps supplemented by other reports in the public domain.

11.6.2 Uncertainty

However, there are other cases where information may be treated as having been made public but final interpretation will depend upon the circumstances. This includes cases where information:

1 *Can be acquired only by exercising diligence or expertise*: this seems to cast some doubt on point (4) above. The doubt seems to relate to the degree of expertise that would be required to tease out the information. A director cannot reasonably depend upon this defence if, in practice, the information was obvious only to insiders and no outsider would be reasonably likely to have deduced it.
2 *It is communicated to a section of the public*: if creditors are aware of a company having difficulty paying its debts, this may not mean that shareholders can be deemed to be aware of it. The director selling shares in these circumstances would probably be held to have had unpublished information.
3 *It can be acquired only by observation*: this is a similar situation to the one in (2) above. If you had to travel to the distant factory to find that there were strike pickets outside the gates, and if the fact had not been reported through newspapers or television then it would seem unreasonable to suppose that the strike was public knowledge. If, on the other hand, large sectors of the public could observe that a bus company was on strike then it would seem reasonable to say it was public information.
4 *It is communicated only on payment of a fee*: if information could only be obtained on payment of a substantial fee and it was not otherwise available then the information could probably not be held to be in the public domain. On the other hand, if it was in a widely read trade journal or a Reuters screen then it probably would be.
5 *It is published only outside the UK*: if news were published in *The Wall Street Journal* then it might be held to be public in the UK but probably not if in *The Ohio Sentinel*.

11.7 DEFENCES

There are a large number of defences against a charge of insider dealing or disclosure (however the burden of proof is placed on the accused):

1 *In the proper performance of one's duties*: disclosure of information in an attempt to conclude a business deal would be acceptable but probably not if it was given to a stockbroker's analyst.
2 *There was no expectation of resultant dealing*: disclosure of information that might fail the test above might nonetheless fall within this

definition but it would be advisable to procure a confidentiality agreement.

A director might seek the reaction of an analyst to a proposal but would have to make them an insider, debarred from dealing or advising on the securities. Not many institutions or individual analysts would volunteer to be put in this position since they could not even act for clients until the information was made public.

3 *If the insider does not expect financial benefit*: this may relate to dealings where the insider can show that it was reasonable to believe that the information would not have a material effect on the price of securities.

4 *The information does not affect the insider's actions*: if the insider can show that he or she would have acted in the same way without access to the information then this is a defence. For example, if the insider needed money to pay a tax bill then they might have sold shares even without knowing that a competitor had just patented a superior product or process.

11.8 AFTERTHOUGHTS

Curiously, deals done on the basis of insider knowledge are neither void nor voidable. This means that someone convicted of a criminal offence under this legislation would still be able to enforce contracts based on their misdeeds.

In practical terms, the risk of prosecution and conviction for insider trading seems very limited, although custom and practice could change at any time. Convictions under the previous insider dealing legislation (superseded in March 1995) have been few and far between, as shown in Table 11.1 below.

	1989/90	1990/91	1991/92	1992/93	1993/94
Convictions	4	0	3	5	2
Acquittals	9	0	5	2	6

Table 11.1: Convictions for insider trading
Source: Department of Trade and Industry

CHAPTER 12

Disciplinary powers of the Exchange

The Exchange has wide discretion, because its rules cannot be expected to be so detailed as to cover every possible problem that may arise.

12.1 POWERS OVER AN ISSUER

The powers of the Exchange over an issuer can be broken down as follows.

12.1.1 Sanctions

If the Exchange considers that an issuer has contravened its rules it may do one or more of the following which are in ascending order of severity.

(a) Fine the issuer. The fact that the issuer has been fined may be published by the Exchange. This would go on the Exchange News Service and would be picked up by member firms and by the press. In any event, the issuer is required to disclose details in their next audited accounts. This sanction is viewed as a lesser penalty and is intended to reinforce the position of the nominated adviser where an issuer fails to heed their advice but resignation is not appropriate.

(b) Censure the issuer. The fact that the issuer has been censured may be published by the Exchange.

(c) Suspend trading or cancel the admission of the issuer's securities. The Exchange has, historically, been reluctant to stop trading in securities because this penalises innocent shareholders as well as the miscreants. The problems for a company arising from criticism alone are quite considerable. Suppliers and customers of the issuer may be influenced, its share price is likely to suffer and its various professional advisers may feel uncomfortable with their association with the issuer. Pressure is likely to be applied, therefore, from a number of quarters to discourage continuation or repetition of the breach of rules.

The Exchange may also suspend trading or cancel the admission of the issuer's securities 'where dealings . . . are not being conducted in an orderly manner or . . .' to protect investors.

12.1.2 Information

The Exchange may require the issuer to provide it with information in any form and may then, if it sees fit, publish that information.

The purpose of these powers is to maintain the smooth operation of the market and to protect investors. The Exchange might, for instance, seek explanations for unusual share price movements or for unusually large share transactions. It might then publish, or oblige the issuer to publish, these reasons (Rules 16.32 and 16.33).

12.2 POWER OVER A DIRECTOR

If the Exchange believes that a contravention of the rules of AIM results from the negligence, omission or positive action of one or more of the directors then the Exchange may:

- censure the relevant directors;
- publish the fact that the directors have been censured (this would go on the Exchange News Service and would be picked up by member firms and by the press);
- publish its opinion that their presence on the board is not in the interests of investors.

This last sanction is reserved for 'persistent or wilful' failure by any director to fulfil their obligations. The term wilful, however, presumably means that it need only be done once – though it does indicate that this sanction could not be applied in cases of error or incompetence.

If the director remained on the board, despite the publishing of this opinion, then the Exchange may suspend trading of the issuer's securities (Rule 16.36.d).

12.3 POWERS OVER NOMINATED ADVISERS AND NOMINATED BROKERS

The powers of the Exchange over nominated advisers and brokers are similar to those applying to issuers. The firm may be censured, with the option of publicising the fact. In more extreme cases, the Exchange may deregister firms. This prevents them acting in this capacity and may also be attended by harmful publicity.

The permitted reasons for applying these sanctions are if:

- an adviser is in breach of its responsibilities (under the AIM Rules);
- the integrity and reputation of the market have been impaired as a result of its conduct or judgement;
- the number of suitably qualified and experienced staff falls below four.

12.4 INFORMAL SANCTIONS

The Exchange may exert powerful informal pressure on companies through their advisers.

As noted above (para **7.1**), an issuer must have a nominated adviser at all times and trading in its securities will be suspended and may be cancelled if it does not have one. In turn, the status of nominated advisers is reviewed annually and their registration may be cancelled 'if the Exchange considers that the integrity and reputation of the market may have been impaired as a result of the conduct or judgement of a nominated adviser . . .'. In addition, the conduct of the nominated adviser will be considered in the light of 'the conduct of companies for which the nominated adviser acts' (Reference: Stock Exchange Requirements for nominated advisers).

There is therefore a pressure on nominated advisers to conform to what the Exchange believes is best practice. There is a risk that if an issuer were to disagree with the opinion of the Exchange and to proceed regardless with a planned course of action, the adviser may feel it necessary to resign. This would leave the issuer to face suspension or cancellation of trading in its securities if it could not find a replacement.

12.5 PROCEDURES

When the Exchange is considering applying sanctions against a party, it will generally give advance notice of its intended action and allow them the opportunity to make representations either in person or in writing. It will then advise them of its decision and give reasons, in writing, for any adverse decisions (Rule 16.38).

The rule includes a caveat that permits the Exchange not to follow this procedure if it considers it would prejudice '. . . an orderly market or the protection of investors . . .'. This would appear to cover circumstances where, for example, an instant suspension of trading in a security is necessary to protect investors in a false market.

12.6 APPEALS

An appeals procedure to an independent panel has been established. This panel comprises individuals who are appointed but not employed by the Exchange. They have a wide range of business experience, including dealings with smaller companies, stock broking and corporate finance.

An appeal may be made by a nominated adviser, a director or an issuer against any disciplinary action of the Exchange. In addition, an issuer may also appeal against any decision of the Exchange arising from the Rules of AIM. Finally, an applicant to become a nominated adviser may appeal against any decision of the Exchange with respect to that application – which would include any conditions imposed as well as outright rejection.

An appeal must be initiated in writing to the secretary to the Appeals Committee. This document must set out the grounds of appeal and principal matters to be relied upon. The published procedures make no reference to any time limit for the lodging of an appeal. Nor do they give a time limit for the hearing of the appeal, nor do they address whether the decision of the Exchange stands in the meantime.

Except in exceptional circumstances, and with the permission of the Appeals Committee ('The Committee'), neither party (the appellant or the Exchange) may present evidence that was not available to those who made the original decision. This focuses the responsibility of the Appeals Committee upon the interpretation of the Rules of AIM and the judgements that lay behind the decisions of the Exchange. If the appellant had, for any reason, not presented relevant facts when the original decision was made then these can be subsequently presented to the Exchange which may, at its absolute discretion, review the decision. If the Exchange declines to do so, then the appellant must initiate an appeal and seek leave to introduce the new evidence to the Appeals Committee as a special case. If this, in turn, is refused then there remains the option of using the courts.

The Appeals Committee has three possible responses to an appeal:

- to overturn the original decision of the Exchange;
- to send the matter back to the Exchange for reconsideration; or
- to reject the appeal.

The Committee itself may not, therefore, amend a decision. While it is unlikely to occur in practice there seems to be a possibility for a dispute to bounce back and forth between the Exchange and the appeal process.

The Committee for each case will comprise five people from a panel appointed by the Exchange and it will be chaired by someone legally qualified. In addition the Committee may co-opt anyone it deems appropriate to the case, which means someone having the particular expertise needed. The appellant may object to individual Committee members if they appear to have any conflict of interest, but this appears to be only at the hearing stage. If this would render the Committee inquorate, the whole procedure would presumably be delayed.

12.6.1 Appeals on applications to become a nominated adviser

An appeal in these circumstances will be by written submissions only. The Exchange will submit its reasons in writing both to the Committee and to the appellant. These reasons will include the basis for the decision and the material facts considered. The appellant will then have the opportunity to respond with any challenge and may add further material facts that may not have been included in the notice of appeal. Both parties may attach copies of relevant documents to their submissions.

12.6.2 Other appeals

For all other appeals, there will be an opportunity for a hearing unless both the Exchange and the appellant agree to dispense with one. The parties may be legally represented and all hearings will be held in private.

As for appeals from prospective nominated advisers cited above, the two sides will send submissions to the Committee and to each other. Having seen the other party's case, each will then say whether they want a pre-hearing review. The purpose of such a review is to clarify understanding of the other party's case and of the facts relied upon. This may involve one or more meetings.

In connection with this clarification process, the Committee may seek schedules to be prepared or documents to be disclosed. It may enquire as to facts relating to the case. It has discretion to set the time and place for pre-hearing reviews to which representatives of the appellant and the Exchange will be invited. The pre-hearing review may be recorded and a transcription made available to the appellant at a cost not exceeding the costs incurred. If either party does not attend, the Committee may proceed in their absence. The Committee also has discretion to set or amend time limits in connection with the review and can make an order for the payment of costs in relation to a pre-hearing review or the preparation involved. The procedures do not specify what costs would be recoverable.

The appellant will receive at least 10 working days notice of the time and place for the hearing itself. The order of proceedings will be at the discretion of the Committee but the appellant will have the right to speak last. The Committee may then deliberate in private and will be able to reach decisions by a majority vote, with the chairman having a casting vote. Any majority decision will not be publicly disclosed. As in the pre-hearing, the appellant will be entitled to a transcription or copy of any record made.

The Committee will put its decision in writing to the appellant and the Exchange covering its findings, the reasons for its decision and any order for costs. The Committee has discretion to make an order for either party to pay reasonable costs that may cover the remuneration and expenses of its members and also any administration costs of the appeal. If awarded, these costs are payable within 10 days (presumably working days) of the issue of the written decision.

The Exchange may publicise the name of the appellant and the terms of the decision, as it deems fit.

CHAPTER 13

Other issues

13.1 JOINING THE OFFICIAL LIST

Once they have traded on AIM for at least two years, companies will be allowed to move to the Official List without having to produce full listing particulars. AIM companies will still have to produce additional information and will need a sponsor, as for a new listing. The detailed regulations governing this transition and requirements for additional information have not yet been published by the Exchange.

This facility will not be effective until 19 June 1997, two years after the opening of AIM.

13.2 FOREIGN COMPANIES

London is, by far, the premier location in the world for the trading in shares of companies operating in other countries. The presence of a sophisticated and active investment community will certainly encourage foreign companies to join AIM. The reduction in post-admission regulation – with its lower cost and reduced administrative burden – of this market is likely to be an added attraction.

Investors must be aware of the fact that, while foreign companies will be subject to all the rules of AIM, they will not come under the jurisdiction of UK company law unless they trade in the UK. While this is no different from foreign companies whose shares trade through the Official List, it may add a little extra risk to a slightly higher risk market. It need present no concern in respect of companies established in most European Community and other countries, which have a generally high standard of investor protection. A particular risk factor would be companies that set up in foreign jurisdictions specifically to avoid scrutiny or control. The history of overseas companies and the reputation of their nominated advisers and brokers will be of particular importance to investors.

The Exchange stipulates no specific requirements for how settlement is to be achieved for AIM companies. It is up to the issuer to establish an appropriate mechanism, which does not have to be carried out in the UK. If carried out in the UK, settlement is covered by the same Exchange rules that apply to domestic securities. The only requirements under the AIM Rules themselves are limited to:

- settlement being completed within 25 days of a trade (Rule 10.2.b); and
- registrars to register a transfer within 14 days of receipt of the transfer document.

Tax reliefs available from investments in AIM, particularly to individual investors, will generally not apply if they are in foreign companies.

The secondary market in trading shares after their initial flotation will depend, to a considerable extent, on the brokers' reports and information published on the company. While this is true for all issuers and not just for overseas ones, it is argued that the foreign company needs to work harder to build up its profile. This makes it particularly important for the overseas company to ensure that its nominated broker will produce and circulate analysis of the company.

13.3 START-UPS

A start-up, in this context, is a business that may have a prototype or product at a pre-production stage and which needs finance to begin trading. We believe that in the early stages of AIM, finance may be hard to raise for a genuine start-up where the assets comprise no more than a management team and an idea. Nonetheless, as investors become more familiar with the market, we can see experienced and impressive management teams raising money to back ideas. This would be direct competition with venture capital finance and may provide a considerable advance on the sources of finance currently available. A similar category of company is the early stage enterprise that is already trading to a limited extent but which requires further finance to expand significantly or, perhaps, to develop products. It is quite likely that AIM will attract some companies in both these categories, particularly high-technology ones. The Official List does provide an exemption from its Rule 3.6 which requires new issues to have a track record of at least three years. However, this is intended for pharmaceutical and medical diagnostic companies which have already attracted funding and have a market value in excess of £20m. It is unlikely that an electronic or computer company would be able to join the Official List as a start-up.

The appetite of investors for such investments will depend upon how the early ones perform and the evidence from the Rule 4.2 Market is that good quality 'high-tech' companies do attract significant investment. Since, by definition, such investments have no track record, the potential investor will be highly influenced by: the reputation of the adviser, broker and any other professional advisers, the background and proven experience of the management team and the degree of commercial support that can be shown. In this last context, the signature of respected consultants through an expert's report may be helpful.

13.4 CORPORATE GOVERNANCE

The Exchange has laid down no rules concerning the internal management processes for companies whose shares are traded on AIM. This is in contrast to the requirement for Official List companies incorporated in the UK, to include in their annual report a statement about whether they have complied with the recommendations of the Committee on the Financial Aspects of Corporate Governance (Rule 12.43.j), published in December 1992. The committee is best known by the name of its chairman, Sir Adrian Cadbury, and its recommended Code of Best Practice is often known as the Cadbury Code. Listed companies are required to state in what ways they may not have complied with the Code and to give reasons.

The absence of regulation, in this matter, is in accordance with the philosophy that AIM should be a lightly regulated market. This does not mean that companies should not aspire to follow the Code. Indeed, investors are likely to see it increasingly as desirable best practice, particularly since the concentration of decision-making on one or two individual directors is likely to be more rather than less common among smaller companies. The City Group for Smaller Companies (CISCO) has published a Guideline for Smaller Companies that seeks to refine the Code to be 'feasible and appropriate' for them. Even this may be onerous for a company capitalised at £10 to £20 m, but it remains, like the Code itself, a target rather than a set of rigid rules. Indeed, paragraph 3.10 of the Code states that:

> 'The Code is to be followed . . . in the light of their own particular circumstances. They are responsible for ensuring that their actions meet the spirit of the Code and in interpreting it they should give precedence to substance over form.'

Investors are likely to be understanding about the difficulties of meeting the full standards initially; they may, for instance, expect only one non-executive director for a small company and would expect the chairman and chief executive roles to be often combined. Nonetheless investors in AIM may actually see the role of the non-executive director as even more important than for larger companies, contributing management wisdom as well as providing some protection for shareholders.

Some of the key points in the Code and the CISCO guidelines that may be helpful for AIM companies are included in Table **13.1** below.

	Cadbury Code	*CISCO Guidelines*
Each company to have non-executive directors 'of sufficient calibre and number for their views to carry significant weight . . .' (the majority to be independent of the company)	3	2

Other issues

	Cadbury Code	*CISCO Guidelines*
Split roles of chief executive and chairman	/	/
Significant matters to be discussed by the whole board as far as practical	/	/
A remuneration committee to consider the pay and benefits of directors and senior managers	Wholly or mainly	Wholly or mainly
An audit committee made up of non-executive directors	Wholly	Mainly
Non-executive directors to serve for a fixed term	/	/
Non-executive directors not to have share options	/	/
Board meetings per annum at least	Not specified	6
Directors' service contracts not to exceed three years without shareholder approval	/	

Table 13.1: Key points in the Cadbury Code and CISCO Guidelines in relation to AIM companies

The Cadbury Code also calls for 'full and clear disclosure' of directors' total emoluments including pension contributions, stock options and performance related payments. A further item, that has led to some debate because it may require extra auditing work, is a requirement for directors to report on the effectiveness of the company's system of internal control. The wording of such a statement will have to be agreed with the auditors. The CISCO recommendations for matters that should be presented to the board are listed in Appendix 6.

13.5 UNCERTAINTY IN THE REGULATIONS

There are a number of instances in which the AIM regulations or their application may be unclear. This arises because it is impossible to cover all the possible situations that may arise. There are therefore significant areas where the Exchange has some discretion over the application of the regulations.

An example of uncertainty arises in Rule 16.27 which deals with the aggregation of transactions since the previous balance sheet date, for the purpose of deciding whether an announcement is required. The sort of transactions this relates to are the buying or selling of substantial assets or other companies. The rule contains one paragraph describing when transactions need to be aggregated and says, 'if together they lead to substantial involvement in a business activity which did not previously form a part of the issuer's principal business activities.'. It may not be at all certain what constitutes 'substantial' nor when an activity is different from a previous principal business activity. If it matters to an issuer whether it comes under an uncertain rule there are two courses of action possible:

1 *Choose a preferred but defensible course of action, and prepare a case to defend it if challenged*: there may be a risk of subsequent challenge, the Exchange taking a contrary view and obliging the issuer to put right the 'error'. The Exchange might even apply sanctions against a company or its directors if it felt they had acted both incorrectly and 'wilfully'.

   If a company can show that it has acted in accordance with professional advice from lawyers, brokers or a nominated adviser then it is unlikely that sanctions could be applied. Such advice would also help to persuade the Exchange. If a decision may be controversial it is always wise, therefore, to be able to demonstrate that good advice has been sought and taken.

   In the light of the informal or indirect powers of the Exchange (see **12.3** above), nominated advisers may prefer to seek guidance from the Exchange rather than risk controversy.

2 *Seek guidance from the Exchange*: the Exchange is usually willing to give informal guidance to companies and their advisers who are uncertain about the interpretation of a regulation in the circumstances they face. The risk to the issuer in seeking this informal guidance directly is that the officials of the Exchange may give guidance that is not the issuer's preferred course of action. The Exchange is then alerted to the matter

and the issuer will need to mount a very strong case, supported by legal advice, for ignoring the guidance they have been given. Even if the issuer makes the approach through an intermediary, it would be difficult for that adviser to collude in ignoring the advice of the Exchange.

PART THREE

The practical issues

CHAPTER 14

Alternatives to AIM

This chapter discusses the alternatives open to directors and shareholders of companies who want to raise new finance or to obtain a trading facility for their shares.

14.1 RULE 4.2

After the introduction of AIM on 19 June 1995, trading in shares by Stock Exchange member firms under Rule 4.2 will change. From September 1995, it will return to being an occasional dealing facility, probably reserved only for suspended securities.

The Exchange has been caught in a dilemma being viewed, by some investors, as responsible for trading in 4.2 stocks despite the fact that they are outside its regulation. The rule, after all, only said that member firms of the Exchange may seek permission to trade in shares off-market. They have resolved this situation by deciding that they will only have any responsibility for trading in shares that really do come under its regulation, anything else is to be truly off-market, with no hint of connection to the Exchange.

There is, of course, nothing to stop future off-market trades, as outlined below, except for problems arising in relation to the Financial Services Act.

14.2 OFF-MARKET

There is nothing to prevent the continuation of share trading outside the jurisdiction of the Stock Exchange. J P Jenkins has announced its intention of continuing to make a market in securities off the Exchange, and has coined a name for this 'market' – Off-Ex. Nonetheless, the majority of trades are likely to be matched bargains. Whoever makes the trade is subject to regulation, as they are currently for trades under Rule 4.2, which is imposed by the Financial Services Act 1986 and by one of the self regulating organisations under that Act, the Securities and Futures Agency (SFA). The SFA has a critical test of the suitability of an investment for a particular client. Therefore any intermediary or broker has to make due enquiry and consider the circumstances of the individual investor. If, for example, 'widows and orphans' were to be persuaded to invest in an unquoted equity there is a high probability that any loss incurred could be recovered from that intermediary. Even if the client was warned of the degree of risk involved, the duty of care placed on the broker would seem to invalidate any disclaimers. The sort of issues that a member of the SFA would be required to consider would include:

- the liquidity of the investment;
- the size of the company invested in;
- the size of the investment;
- the degree of concentration of the investor's resources.

There is a presumption that the degree of risk grows the further away one gets from blue chip stocks on the Official List.

The financial intermediary or broker is therefore under considerable risk if they introduce non-quoted securities to investors for whom they are unsuitable. The only investor who might sensibly be considered would be what is termed a sophisticated investor which excludes all but professional people or those who have proven experience of having invested widely in unquoted stocks.

Another significant deterrent to off-market dealing may be a lack of published prices. At present trades under Rule 4.2 are published along with the Daily Official List. *The Financial Times* then publishes these prices on a Saturday. After 29 September 1995, trading under Rule 4.2 will cease except for limited circumstances and the Exchange will no longer publish transaction prices. A service called the Non-SEAQ Noticeboard, run by the RNS and Newstrack (part of J P Jenkins), currently allows brokers to post a price for buy or sell orders of securities traded under Rule 4.2. This will also be discontinued at the end of September 1995. Brokers or market makers may, however, find a way to publish the prices of trades, possibly in the FT or possibly electronically. The Internet may well provide a cheap and easy means for brokers to publish information of this sort to anyone who has a computer and a modem. There will be a continuing problem in knowing which price is the 'market price' since transactions may go through different brokers at different prices. The brokers may not know about these other bargains, since it is the market function to co-ordinate prices. This fragmentation makes it impossible for a broker to guarantee that the best possible buying or selling price will be achieved for a client off-market. It is possible that this problem may be addressed by someone offering an electronic noticeboard, in succession to the Non-SEAQ Noticeboard, on the Internet.

Although firm data is hard to come by, we believe that around 50 institutions invest in shares traded on the 4.2 Market. However most of these will be more reluctant or may be unable to trade in shares that have no continuously available price quoted. The off-market trading is therefore likely to be mainly confined to wealthy individuals and private client funds.

The very existence of AIM may make investors think of off-market transactions as slightly disreputable and some brokers will be reluctant to be involved. However, it will provide a very useful trading facility for less liquid shares, where there is no strong reason to seek a more formal facility. Investors in companies whose shares trade in this way would have the protection of the Companies Act and the Financial Services Act but may not receive:

- interim reports;
- announcements of significant transactions;
- announcements of transactions with directors or connected parties.

Also the directors would not have to observe the Exchange's Model Code for directors' share dealings. It is possible that a broker or market maker dealing in this market may themselves impose conditions on companies who may want a dealing facility. Such conditions might mirror some of the Exchange's requirements.

As noted above, the market rule that requires brokers to achieve best advantage for their client (the best price in all the circumstances) cannot apply off-market and nor would the Stock Exchange compensation fund cover such investors in the event of the collapse of a broker.

The very existence of dealing off-market may encourage issuers whose securities are less liquid to prefer this 'market' and not join AIM. The result would be a boost to the integrity and reputation of AIM.

14.3 VENTURE CAPITAL

Venture capital institutions are unusual in that the funds may themselves be investors in AIM (through venture capital trusts and also directly), they may use the market as a potential exit route for their investment, they may invest in parallel with a fundraising through AIM and they themselves provide an alternative source of funding to a flotation.

For the shareholders in a company that seeks to raise finance and has a view to an eventual flotation, venture capital funding may be more expensive than an issue on AIM. There are two broad reasons for this:

1 Venture capitalists seek rates of return that are frequently as high as 30 to 35% per annum to provide them with an adequate return for the degree of risk they take.

   A part of this risk is that they are tied in to an illiquid investment and they have taken on a high proportion of the risk in that company. A flotation on AIM automatically overcomes this problem of being 'locked-in' but only up to a point. It may not be easy for a large investor in a company that is facing trading difficulties to find a buyer for their shares.

2 There is a continuing cost of managing venture capital funds, which is typically 2.5% of the funds under management.

   A company that is raising funds will probably have paid heavier up-front costs in the form of fees to professional advisers and intermediaries but, we believe, the 'running return' to investors will be lower than venture capitalists require. At the same time, they will have achieved their longer-term goal of a listing – albeit not on the Official List. They have also provided an exit route for both original and new investors, a way for the original investors to value their holding and to turn some of their effort into cash as well as providing the kudos of a listing.

For a variety of reasons, many companies will not be suitable for AIM. For example:

1 Company too small: many companies that seek new funding will be too small to raise funds through AIM economically. It appears unlikely that it will make economic sense for companies seeking to raise less than £0.75m of new money to do so through AIM since it appears very unlikely that the cost can be reduced below around £70,000. We believe that companies are generally unlikely to be willing to pay more than 10% of sums raised in fees. For smaller companies it may therefore be more economical to seek venture capital funding.
2 Unwilling to accept up-front costs.
3 Management want to remain private: while there is a low regulatory burden on management, they may prefer to carry on their affairs out of the limelight. They will have to accept, however, disclosure requirements to the venture capitalists that will be at least as demanding as those to AIM investors.
4 Unable to interest brokers: there will certainly be economic sectors that will be unfashionable and will not be attractive to brokers. In such cases it may prove easier to attract a single venture capital institution than to communicate with several hundred potential 'retail investors'.

There may be opportunities for companies to raise finance both from venture capital institutions and from AIM. The most common will be where initial finance is provided by venture capitalists and further rounds of finance through AIM. However, it is possible that initial finance may be provided by these institutions investing through AIM, or in parallel with AIM investors.

14.4 BUSINESS ANGELS

The term business angel derives from the investors in new theatrical productions who are termed 'angels', perhaps in gratitude. A business angel is, similarly, a private investor who takes a stake in the business in return for funding. Research has indicated that the business angels are sometimes friends, acquaintances and family but often they are successful entrepreneurs who have spare cash available to invest in other entrepreneurs. Typically these investments are made in businesses that are located close to where the investors live. These angels are likely to seek an active involvement in the business, which may lead to the useful transfer of skills but also to potential tensions and conflict with the founders.

As with venture capital funding, the business angels provide a partial solution to companies seeking finance for growth. They too will seek an exit, which will come from a trade sale, flotation, refinancing or re-purchase of their shares by the founders. AIM offers not just new funding but also a route for investors to sell their shares, therefore providing a possible exit. This may be particularly appropriate to business angels who may find the tax reliefs helpful to their circumstances eg the ability to carry over capital gains into new investments.

14.5 OVERSEAS EXCHANGES

Except for special circumstances such as a company conducting a large proportion of its business in another country, there seems little obvious attraction to listing outside the UK. The objective of the European Community Listing Directive was to bring standards and requirements closer together throughout the Community. It is therefore unlikely that a company can escape regulatory requirements by listing elsewhere; costs are therefore likely to be similar and it would be surprising if there were more active investors outside the UK, which has by far the most active stock market in the Community. For comparison, in 1994 the turnover in foreign stocks on the London Stock Exchange was £359 bn, compared with £12 bn in Germany and £2.5 bn in Paris. Even the New York Stock Exchange transacts less than half the amount of foreign business that London does.

14.5.1 NASDAQ

The American National Association of Securities Dealers (NASD) has 5,694 members (1991), comprising virtually all those who deal with the public. It set up the automated quotation system (NASDAQ) in 1971, seeing an opportunity to satisfy the public interest in owning shares in smaller, rapidly growing companies, in an economic way. The Association recognised that the floor based securities markets such as the New York and American Stock Exchanges (NYSE and AMEX) were not ideally suited to trading the shares of smaller companies. Transactions in shares in these companies are generally in smaller parcels, have a lower aggregate value and are less frequent than transactions in the stock of large companies. Yet the cost of a large trade is very similar to a small one under these systems, while a less frequently traded stock leads to a larger risk to the market maker in quoting a firm price.

Shares in smaller companies are attractive to those who seek unusually high returns; it is easier to double the value of shares in a company with a turnover of £500,000 than to do the same with one of £5bn. This follows because it only takes one successful innovation or investment by the smaller firm to create enough value to make a significant impact, whereas the larger enterprise will need many very substantial successes to achieve the same thing. Jim Slater's much quoted remark sums up this situation, '. . . elephants don't gallop . . .'.

The American National Association of Securities Dealers innovated through allowing each member to make its own bid and offer prices and to publish them through a computer system. This allowed others to compare prices and so introduced competition between all these market makers. The typical stock is reported to have no less than 12 market makers, though the Pareto principle also applies, with 20% of them accounting for 80% of the volume. The automated system that has no physical location, just communication between computers, has also offered a lower cost dealing system. Clearly it worked, since NASDAQ has become the fifth largest securities market worldwide, accounting for approximately 42% of US share turnover. It had a capitalisation of £166bn at the end of 1992 and listed 4,113 companies – more than on any other exchange worldwide. Listing on NASDAQ is available to companies with a net worth in excess of $2m and assets in excess of $4m.

The market operates in two tiers, called the National Market and the SmallCap Market, the latter of which imposes less demanding listing requirements. The comparison is shown in Table 14.1 below.

	*National Market** $	*SmallCap Market* $
Total assets	4m	4m
Total equity		2m
Minimum public float	500,000	100,000
Market value of float	3m	1m
Number of shareholders	400+	300
Minimum share price	5	3
Number of market makers	2	2

* These conditions apply to a company producing a pre-tax profit in excess of £750,000 – more stringent conditions apply to 'research and development companies not yet showing a profit'.

Table 14.1: National Market and SmallCap Market

NASDAQ operates a screen based quote driven system supported by over 400 market makers.

Particularly for 'high tech' companies and especially for those which do a substantial amount of business in the USA, NASDAQ is a market that offers considerable attractions. Even for overseas shares in these categories it can offer greater liquidity and more potential investors than the UK market for smaller companies. It is clear that some venture capital houses will favour NASDAQ over AIM for their companies which trade internationally.

14.5.2 EASDAQ

EASDAQ stands for European Association of Securities Dealers Automated Quotation. The promoters are seeking to raise money to start this new pan-European exchange which is planned to open in 1996. It is no accident that the name is similar to the North American version, NASDAQ, since the latter is one of the bodies much involved in the development in Europe. The proponents of EASDAQ see it as the European version of NASDAQ, attracting high technology and rapidly growing companies as well as those with too short a track record to join a national stock exchange. This exchange will be as highly regulated as the Official List in London and therefore flotation on this market is not intended to be a significantly cheaper option.

The idea is that the new exchange will attract a wider and therefore larger pool of capital than has been available for any single country's second tier market. The argument is made that no single national market within the European Union can provide sufficient numbers of good investment opportunities or of potential investors in order to achieve a critical mass. This is put forward as the reason for the repeated failures of second markets in Europe, while it may explain the success of NASDAQ – which has achieved critical mass through serving a large population of investors.

Clearly this concept is attractive to the continental stock exchanges which see more business in the shares of their resident companies taking place in London than in their own countries. This happens in all the European states except for Germany. The continental traders therefore see EASDAQ as an opportunity to win back some of that business. Many UK observers had supported EASDAQ initially because they were unhappy about the closure of the USM, without immediate replacement, and then with the draft regulations for AIM. The London Stock Exchange has responded to those criticisms, which centred on a perception of an excessive lack of regulation. Many potential advisers, financiers and brokers felt that if regulation were too light the market would attract too many poor investments, which would deter investors and lead to the failure of the market. The new rules appear to satisfy many of the UK critics, which will encourage them to support AIM.

The question then is whether there is enough business for both AIM and EASDAQ. While only time can tell, we feel it is unlikely, if AIM succeeds, that such a close competitor will also succeed. It is hard to see what advantage international fund managers and brokers will gain from dealing on EASDAQ compared with AIM, except for giving the satisfaction of not trading through London. They would be able to achieve the same liquidity by having direct access to the large pool of international financial specialists either located in or trading through London. Indeed it is UK based institutions that are best known, at present, for cross-border investment. Figures for 1991 show London having more overseas banks established there than any other financial centre in the world – 527 banks from 76 countries. It is the world's largest foreign exchange centre, the primary centre for international bond issuance and trading and the world's leading centre for trading overseas equities[1]. Therefore the success of EASDAQ would require many institutions which are based or have establishments in London to prefer its offering to AIM and the London Stock Exchange.

While particular investment opportunities may attract UK investors, there seem insufficient positive reasons for them actively to seek opportunities on EASDAQ. This poses the question whether funds follow good investment opportunities or whether the dynamic companies follow the funds they need to grow. If EASDAQ were to acquire a better reputation than AIM, perhaps as a result of some corporate failures, then the rapidly growing companies might see the pan-European market as the one to be listed on. In that case, if the investors followed them then EASDAQ would gain a momentum and might prove the dominant exchange.

As European integration proceeds, there may be some move towards a merging of national exchanges in the same way as the regional exchanges within the UK merged. However, it is worth noting that the London Stock Exchange is pursuing more local rather than national or supra-national initiatives. The Exchange sees marketing by UK regional brokers of local firms to local investors as a particular opportunity for AIM. If this proves successful it would not seem a good augury for a pan-European ideal.

14.6 THE OFFICIAL LIST

The Official List is obviously an alternative to and a competitor of AIM. Figure 14.1 below shows the large number of smaller companies that have opted to join the Official List over the years despite the availability of the USM and the Third Market. Since 1987 a varying proportion of the companies joining the Official List have had a market capitalisation of less than £50m. At its lowest, this proportion has been 55% of the total number of new issues: at its highest it has been 74% of the new issues. Indeed, the Official List has attracted a steady stream even of companies with a market capitalisation of less than £10m. In the late 1980s (before the announcement of the closure of the USM) the number of companies

[1] Data quoted by the Corporation of London.

with a market capitalisation of less than £10m which joined the Official List was between a half and a third of the number joining the USM in any year.

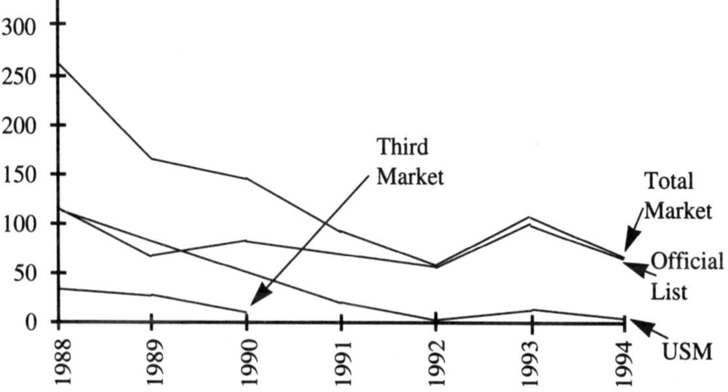

Figure 14.1: Number of new issues on the London Stock Exchange with market capitalisation less than £50m
Source: London Stock Exchange Quarterly Reviews

Some directors will feel that their companies attain greater prestige by joining the Official List rather than any second tier market. This would appear to be the only real advantage of the Official List for these smaller companies, since the SEATS trading system will be common to all AIM companies and to those on the Official List which have fewer than two market makers. On the other hand, the attraction of AIM should be: a lower cost to join and for continuing membership, tax advantages for investors and, most importantly, greater visibility and interest in AIM shares compared with the 'bottom end' of the Official List. The small companies that join the Official List are liable to find that there is very little trading in their securities and that it is not easy to issue further shares to raise further capital.

The key factors that will encourage companies to prefer AIM are therefore going to be the prestige that AIM is able to attract in the early years of its existence and the investor interest in shares on the new market. With its own dedicated management team, something that previous second tier markets in London lacked, there are very good prospects for building and maintaining this interest.

Depending upon how AIM develops over the long term, companies may see it as a stepping stone to the Official List or to other exchanges such as NASDAQ. If AIM develops its own strong following, companies may prefer to remain on it rather than transferring to the Official List. Indeed, in such circumstances there are clear advantages to remaining on AIM and little obvious reason to switch to the Official List with its greater demands. However, the tax advantages apply to AIM securities on the understanding that it is an 'unlisted' market. If it includes many large companies with very active trading in their shares then this status might be at risk and pressure may grow for larger companies to transfer to the Official List.

14.7 TRADEPOINT

At the time of writing, Tradepoint has received authorisation from the Securities and Investment Board, which is awaiting confirmation from the Treasury. Its directors hope to provide a screen based system for institutional investors to deal directly with each other, cutting out the intermediation of a broker. It will be an order driven system; an institution will enter a buy or sell order at a specified price and anyone interested in providing the other side of the transaction just has to press a key to execute the trade, which is totally anonymous. This anonymity may be important for some large investors who feel that the market price moves against them when it is known they are interested in a security.

For smaller companies with fewer and more irregular trades in their shares, transactions will take place at periodic auctions, from a few hours to a week apart. All bids and offers entered since the last auction will then be cleared.

The system is essentially one for dealing and settlement rather than being an alternative exchange providing regulation, such as the London Stock Exchange. It may be seen as an alternative to SEAQ and SEATS therefore, rather than as a rival to AIM. Indeed it will be financed largely by a levy on the value of trades.

CHAPTER 15

Joining AIM

This chapter covers the main logistical issues involved in joining AIM; what route to pursue to have shares admitted to trading on the market and the detailed steps that are necessary. In covering the steps to admission, we cover the transitional arrangements for companies joining from 4.2 and the USM. The procedures for joining either from the Official List or from the USM will be the same. The final matter of importance that we discuss is the cost of joining.

15.1 METHODS OF JOINING AIM

There are four basic techniques for achieving admission to a stock exchange, although there are many variations of these. The first three are: an introduction, a placing and a public offer. Between 1980 and 1990 a total of 740 companies joined the USM as follows:

Placing	70%
Introduction	18%
Offer for sale	10%
	98%

The balance of 2% entered through provisions of Rule 163 which made them similar to an introduction. Even these figures understate the apparent attractions of placing since the Exchange's restrictions were changed in 1986 to allow USM companies to raise larger sums through this technique.

In addition, the statistics for introductions were boosted by 30 transfers from the Third Market in the year preceding its closure.

The use of placing in initial public offers appears to be largely related to cost considerations. Research was published by the Stock Exchange[1] in 1991 which related directly to the costs associated with different methods of flotation. It raised three issues in particular:

1 There is a significant fixed cost to flotation, regardless of the amount of new investment raised. This results in the costs associated with raising less than £1m in the initial public offer being over 20% of the amount of money raised – falling to 6% by the time more than £10m is raised.
2 There does appear to be a cost differential between the methods of flotation, with an offer for sale costing around 1 to 2% more than a placing.
3 The discount on new issues is a significant (but perhaps seldom considered) element of their cost. The 'discount' is the extent to which the price increases in the market immediately after the issue. Generally a company and its advisers will aim to issue new securities for a little less than they are expected to be priced by the market. The instant profit that results will encourage potential purchasers and stimulate trading in the securities. This is therefore just another cost of the issue. Placings appear, on average, to be a little more 'underpriced' than offers for sale.

The fourth method of admission to a stock exchange is different in kind – it is a reverse takeover and all four methods are now discussed in detail below.

15.1.1 Introduction

An introduction occurs when shares are admitted to trading but no new shares are issued. A prospectus is not required although the Admission Document must be available to the public on enquiry. This method is suitable when the issuer has no immediate need for new funding or wider share ownership, although a share issue will often follow later.

---

[1] 'Costs of Capital raising on the USM', Stock Exchange Quarterly – Autumn 1991.

15.1.2 Placing

A placing is a sale of securities to a small group of investors, in contrast to an offer to the public at large. The issuing house technically underwrites the share issue on 'impact day' some five days before trading commences. However, they will usually expect to have placed the issue with investors on the same day, so their risk is limited. Sometimes investors may be invited to bid for shares within a price range in a process called book building. The Official List requires a minimum of 100 placees and, for companies with a market capitalisation between £25m and £50m, there is an additional requirement that no more than 75% of the issue can be placed. The balance must be sold to a wider market through a public offering or through intermediaries to their clients (termed an intermediaries offer). There is no similar requirement for shares traded on AIM to be spread in this way and a placing is likely to prove the most popular means of joining the market for the two main reasons detailed below:

1. With a placing, the issuer does not underwrite the issue (although there is a placing fee) there is no logistical process of advertising and distributing many prospectuses, a relatively small number of potential investors can be visited by the management team and the overall cost may prove lower than for a public offer.
2. If some shareholders are selling then they may find it easier to avoid having to make a responsibility statement as an offeror of securities.

There is a third reason, which only applies to a minority of companies. In these cases brokers will advise that a public offer may not appeal to private investors. They may argue that the industry or the particular business is hard for unsophisticated investors to understand. There are a number of examples from recent experience. One is a company whose prime activity is owning and operating casinos in the UK and abroad. This was viewed as an investment carrying higher than average risk and it joined the market through a placing. In another case, a very successful company providing venture capital joined the Official List through an offer for sale to the public despite widespread press comment that it was a 'share for the professionals'. We believe there is more mythology than fact in these judgements as to how easily a company can be understood by private investors. Private investors seem well able to assess these matters and shares in both the companies referred to above rose significantly in their first year of flotation. We believe that private investors too are interested in good investments.

Placing has been the most frequently used method of admission to the USM, with institutions frequently selling-on shares into their individual funds or to private clients. The disadvantage of a placing may be that the resulting shareholder base is too narrow, with ensuing weak trading in the shares. This, in turn, could lead to a reduced share price reflecting poor liquidity and hence further fund raising through the market might be more difficult or more expensive.

15.1.3 Offer for sale

A public offer is a sale of securities, at a fixed price, directly to the public through advertising, press reports and marketing to institutional investors and private client stockbrokers. This method requires active promotion to potential opinion formers such as journalists and stockbrokers' analysts. A version of this offer process is a sale through intermediaries who can sell-on to their clients. The public offer will generally achieve a wider spread of shareholding than alternatives but the cost of promoting the issue will probably be greater than for a placing.

There are means of distributing shares that are a combination of the two underlying methods. One is a placing and public offer, another allows a 'clawback' of shares placed with institutions if there is sufficient demand from the public offer. Underlying the decision behind which method of distribution to choose are the director's objectives and a view of who the likely investors will be. If directors of an issuer seek to achieve a wide spread of shareholders and an active aftermarket then a public offer is more likely to achieve this than a placing. However it is too early to tell whether private investors in AIM shares will have a greater tendency to hang on to their shares compared with the USM and Official List.

15.1.4 Reverse takeover

In a reverse takeover a company which wants a listing arranges to be taken over by another whose shares are already traded on an exchange. The buyer issues its shares as payment. The shareholders in the acquired company generally end up with having the majority of shares in the merged company and their management are in control.

The rules of AIM will demand the suspension of share trading and a new Admission Document in many of these cases (see Chapter 9).

15.1.5 Underwriting

Public offers on the Official List are largely underwritten. Underwriting is a process whereby the underwriter contracts to buy any shares not taken up in the initial offer. The underwriter will pass on some of the risk to sub-underwriters who also take a fee. A proportion of initial offerings on AIM may not be underwritten. In such cases, the POS Regulations demand that a document falling under them (any Admission Document) must state the minimum amount to be raised. There will certainly be a class of shares, like the former BES schemes, where if the target fund raising is not met then the flotation is abandoned. Certainly the evidence of research carried out by Paul Marsh at the London Business School is that the costs of underwriting give more than a fair return to the underwriters. Over time this is bound to have an effect on the popularity of the process, which takes a high proportion of flotation costs. At around 2.25% of the sum raised, a £10m fund raising might cost £200,000 in advisory fees etc and £225,000 in underwriting fees.

15.1.6 Detailed steps to admission

Decision to seek admission

The directors' decision to join AIM will result from wider discussions. They will identify their objectives and consider the alternative means to attain them.

Appointment of advisers etc

The following appointments will need to be considered:

1 *Nominated adviser and nominated broker*: as discussed previously, these roles may be covered by the same firm.

2 *Solicitors*: while most companies will use their existing solicitors, it is important that the legal advisers have experience of corporate finance matters and of public documents.

3 *Security printers*: the choice of printers will depend upon the price they quote and the level of their other business at the time. It will also be strongly influenced by the advisers and who they have worked with in the past.

4 *Public relations company*: not all smaller companies use financial PR consultants. However, they can be very useful in liaising with opinion formers in the financial press, with brokers' analysts and continuing to get the management's message across after a flotation. Their services are probably not cost-effective when a company joins AIM through a small placing of, say £1m to £5m, with a handful of institutions. In such circumstances, the company's broker will be able to get its message across to the small number of key decision makers, while few brokers' analysts will be willing to follow a company which is likely to have little trading in its shares. The cost of retaining one of the leading consultancies for a smaller company flotation is likely to be between £25,000 and £40,000 depending upon the particular circumstances. A continuing retainer may cost between £8,000 and £15,000 per annum.

Agree method of admission

The method of admission will influence other matters and must be decided at an early stage. The advantages and disadvantages of different routes are discussed elsewhere.

Accountants' engagement letter

The contents of this letter will be a result of decisions taken about the method of admission and the degree and scope of due diligence required. It is subject to negotiation between the issuer, its advisers and reporting accountants. Its content will depend upon the circumstances of each individual company. The time taken by the accountants to complete their work and its cost will depend upon the size of company, scope of work and whether it has been planned to coincide with the annual audit.

Presentations to institutions

The choice of institutions to meet and the form of the presentation to them are important steps in the flotation process. Such a presentation explains why potential investors should invest in the company and it is covered by the same legal obligations as a prospectus – it must contain all necessary information and must not be misleading. The presentation notes and any slides should be included in the verification process.

Drafting of Admission Document

The Admission Document will be drafted and revised many times over a two- to three-week period. The original draft is usually produced by the adviser, possibly working with descriptive text provided by the issuer.

Verification of Admission Document

See para **5.6**.

Directors' statements

There are a number of directors' statements required which are summarised in para **6.5**.

Pricing

The pricing of the share issue will usually be accomplished in two steps. At a very early stage the nominated adviser and the nominated broker will give a price range based upon their research and knowledge of the business. Clearly, at this stage, the issuer may decide not to proceed if the range is unsatisfactory. As the date for admission approaches, the price will be discussed between advisers and issuer in the light of market conditions and early responses from potential institutional investors. The final pricing meeting usually takes place just before the Admission Document is sent for printing.

15.2 JOINING AIM FROM OTHER MARKETS

There are a number of other markets from which a company can move to AIM. In addition, there is no reason why a company whose securities already trade on a recognised exchange (for example, the second market of another European Union country) could not also seek a trading facility on AIM as well.

15.2.1 European Community

The Investment Services Directive of the European Union comes into force in 1996. One of its purposes is to permit companies trading on one exchange in the European Community to be able to gain admission to trading on another. The Prospectus Directive (89/298/EEC) requires that a prospectus approved in one country may be used in another with minor adjustments to reflect issues of local taxation, arrangements for paying agents, notices etc. This provision only applies to companies seeking a listing on another exchange within the European Community within three months of their original listing.

15.2.2 The Official List

If companies whose shares trade on the Official List decide to move to AIM, perhaps because the visibility of smaller companies proves to be greater on that market or to take advantage of the tax reliefs available to investors, the transition will not require an Admission Document.

15.3 TRANSITIONAL ARRANGEMENTS

15.3.1 Rule 4.2

The Exchange has announced that trading under Rule 4.2 will cease at the close of business on 29 September 1995. This will allow companies just over three months after the opening of AIM to decide whether to seek admission to the new market. Those companies whose securities traded under Rule 4.2 on 1 May 1995 will benefit from transitional arrangements which will reduce the requirements for admission.

The transitional arrangements allow the use of a simplified Admission Document. However, if a company is taking advantage of the move to AIM to issue further shares it may still need to produce a prospectus that meets the requirements of the Companies Act or of the Public Offer of Securities Regulations 1995 (if they are in force at the time).

The main elements of the simplified Admission Document are:

- details of the issuer's securities and share capital;
- details of the issuer's activities;
- a comment on recent developments and prospects for the current year;
- the most recent annual accounts. (If more than nine months have elapsed since the end of the financial year then unaudited interim accounts are required in addition);
- working capital statement. (A statement from the directors that the company has sufficient working capital to meet its present requirements will mean that an accountant's report to support this will be needed.)

The differences, compared with the full admission procedures, appear to be:

1 Only one year's accounts required rather than three and no additional statement on them from the auditors or accountant's report.
2 There appears to be no general duty of disclosure as demanded for a normal Admission Document . . . [the document to contain] . . . 'all such information as investors would reasonably require and reasonably expect to find there for the purpose of making an informed assessment . . .' (POS Regulations 1995 para 9). This should significantly reduce the amount of due diligence required.

15.3.2 USM

Companies joining AIM from the USM will be required only to:

- deliver an undertaking to abide by the rules of AIM;
- have appointed nominated advisers and nominated brokers;
- pay the admission fees to AIM.

They will not be required to produce an Admission Document. Indeed there is no formal requirement to send a circular to investors, although it would be surprising if companies did not do this. As well as the additional tax benefits arising for investors from having shares traded on AIM (see **16.2**), there is also the disadvantage that they would no longer be eligible for inclusion in Personal Equity Plans.

15.4 COSTS

The costs of obtaining a trading facility on AIM are likely to vary widely depending upon the circumstances of the issuer, what they are trying to achieve and the advisers they choose. For example, where a company is raising finance it is likely to incur higher costs than if it is only obtaining a simple trading facility. Where a company is a start-up, there is likely to be less to investigate than if it is long-established or has a complex organisation, and it will probably therefore incur lower costs.

There will also be considerable competition and difference of approach between advisers; some will insist upon very thorough and wide ranging due diligence. They will argue that only such high standards will protect their own good name and also attract sufficient interest from investors to obtain the funds and wide aftermarket that is sought. Other advisers will seek more of a commercial due diligence or may feel that a more focussed and less wide ranging investigation will provide perfectly adequate protection to themselves and to investors. Some advisers will demand their own legal representation at all drafting meetings (paid for by the issuer) while others will feel that one set of solicitors representing the company will suffice.

It is incumbent upon issuers joining AIM to talk to a number of potential advisers and to compare their costs and what those costs will achieve. On the one hand, lower costs may not produce the best long-term result, which is a fully subscribed share issue and a wide spread of supportive investors who will invest further in the growth of the business. On the other hand, an issuer may be mistaken in thinking that a high cost or a well-known house necessarily implies a better job for all circumstances.

The costs divide into two broad areas: what it takes to gain admission and what it takes to fulfil continuing obligations.

15.4.1 Initial costs

The initial costs will vary dramatically, depending upon the type of admission that is sought. The two broad categories are the obtaining of a trading facility with or without an associated fund raising. The former can be achieved very cheaply.

Trading facility without fund raising

For a company that is not seeking to raise new funds, the obligations to obtain admission to AIM are very light and could be satisfied with a little extra work by the auditors at the time the annual accounts are produced. The resulting Admission Document does not need to be circulated to existing shareholders. The additional work by lawyers and brokers would then be minimal and the cost might be only a few thousand pounds.

The issue for the company directors is to wonder what they have achieved if they produce minimal information. Will anyone actually trade in their shares other than the small group of existing shareholders? Companies that have produced a prospectus in the recent past, such as many of those trading currently under the Stock Exchange Rule 4.2, will find a market for their shares even if they produce little extra information. For others, particularly if they have a short trading record, it may be far more difficult. Some companies may obtain a following as a result of write-ups in the magazines and newsletters that are beginning to follow the 'unlisted' market. Some of the institutional investors that carry out their own company visits, investigation and appraisal may not be too concerned by the lack of a prospectus and a reporting accountant. But there are, at present, only a handful of specialist, smaller company funds of this type.

In summary, a company seeking only to continue an existing trading facility will be able to do so very cheaply. One seeking to widen its shareholder base and to encourage more active trading will probably need to produce a fuller document which could be circulated to brokers and prospective shareholders.

The cost of moving to AIM from the USM or Official List should be a few hundred pounds since there is virtually nothing to do. However, as most companies following this route will want to write to inform shareholders of what they have done, this will be an extra cost.

The cost of moving to AIM from the Rule 4.2 trading facility will not be significantly less than for a new company joining without raising new funds. The only substantial concession in the transitional arrangements is a reduced requirement for historical financial information.

Trading facility with fund raising

The consensus from the larger brokers is that they expect to see a similar level of enquiry carried out for AIM as for the Official List and the cost of the flotation is likely to be 60 to 70% of a full listing. Because the companies joining AIM will tend to be smaller than those going on to the Official List, they are also likely to have fewer subsidiaries and divisions, making the accountants' reports easier and cheaper. A total cost, depending on the amount raised, of anywhere between £100,000 to £350,000 should therefore be expected on this basis.

Costs of the higher level will be disproportionate to a fund raising of, say, £1m. Our research suggests that there is recognition that it is inappropriate for fees to be more than 10 to 15% of the sum raised in such circumstances. There are firms who would be willing to undertake the work for a cost of this order: the unanswerable question is whether investors will have a lesser confidence in such issues.

The costs will be lower for a number of reasons:

1 *Less work required*: the broker will not need to negotiate with the Stock Exchange over the Admission Document, there will be no checklist against the requirements of the Yellow Book for listing particulars and there will be no need to publish consultants' reports. In respect of this last point, the nominated advisers may want a report from independent experts but, if it is not published with the attendant liability, one would expect the consultants to charge less.

   Some brokers will also be content with commercial due diligence and a reporting accountant's short form report rather than the full and more expensive long form report. This may save substantial sums, since a long form report will generally cost in excess of £20,000 and may cost more than £50,000.

2 *Less duplication*: since the nominated adviser will generally not have legal responsibility for the document, there seems no reason for them to be legally represented, removing a significant element of cost.

3 *Lower charge rates*: the brokers expect advisers to quote lower prices than for Official List flotations, for similar work, which poses the question of why the work cannot be done more cheaply on the Official List.

We expect that the minimum cost for an admission that includes fund raising, will be of the order of £75,000 to £100,000.

Accounting for costs

The Financial Reporting Standard 4 (FRS 4) splits costs associated with a flotation into two categories: those relating to the issue of new shares and those relating to listing on an exchange (which includes joining AIM). It permits the costs associated with issuing new shares to be deducted from the share premium account relating to those new shares. A share premium account arises from shares being issued at a price higher than the nominal value. If shares with a nominal value of, say, £1 are issued at a higher price of, say, £2.50 then the issued share capital account is credited with £1 per share and the share premium account with the balance of £1.50. Note that company law does not ordinarily permit shares to be issued at a lower price than the nominal value.

However, FRS 4 requires costs associated with the listing to be deducted from the profit & loss account of the year. It is not always clear which category a particular cost falls into and it is natural for an issuer to try to allocate costs to the share issue rather than the listing. Since AIM companies will generally be smaller than those on the Official List, these listing costs will be a relatively higher proportion of profits. The directors of an issuer might therefore feel that their published profits were greatly distorted by FRS 4. However, if these costs are disclosed clearly then we argue that it should not make any significant difference to investors.

Taxes

VAT will be payable on professional and other fees associated with a new share issue. However, they will not be recoverable against the input VAT of the business, whereas those associated with the listing will be recoverable. The principle is that VAT charged on raising capital is not associated with trading and therefore cannot be recovered against VAT paid out on trading expenses.

15.4.2 Continuing costs

One of the most significant attractions of AIM, compared with the Official List, is the lighter continuing obligations. For example, unless a company completely changes its trade within a 12-month period it will have to do no more than notify its shareholders of acquisitions. This compares with the heavy obligations and costs (of several hundred thousand pounds) of a Super Class One Circular that might be necessary for a company to make a significant acquisition when its shares trade on the Official List.

This lower level of cost is a particular attraction to a relatively small company, say with a market capitalisation of £10m to £20m, growing rapidly by acquisition. For them, expenditure that might easily be £300,000 on a circular (including a working capital report and indebtedness statement) would seem hard to justify.

Of course, directors who wish to raise more money from shareholders in order to finance acquisitions will still have to provide significant information. What is required will evolve with the market and should be driven by investors rather than advisers.

Other areas of cost are the fees paid to the nominated adviser and (if different) the nominated broker. The Exchange sets no guidelines for these, which are subject to negotiation and will depend upon the tasks the issuer asks its advisers to perform. For example, the issuer may wish its nominated broker to produce reports for investors, it may want the broker to act as a liaison with major shareholders etc. With the wide variety of firms eligible to become nominated advisers and the essentially reactive role the Exchange perceives for them, these fees should not be a disincentive to joining AIM. The continuing level of fees also depends upon how active the issuer is. For example, a broker acting for an inactive client may charge £2,500 to £5,000 per annum while a company that rings the broker every day and issues new shares or makes acquisitions may pay £10,000 to £15,000 per annum.

It is possible that some market makers will request retainers in order to make firm prices, though the main market makers are not contemplating this at present.

CHAPTER 16

Investing in AIM securities

The most important issue for any market, whether taking place in a town square or across computer links, is who will buy the produce. A stock market is no different from a vegetable market in this respect and the interests of an investing community are paramount to the success of AIM. In this chapter we discuss the investors in AIM and the tax reliefs that are available to them.

16.1 THE INVESTORS

Who will be the investors in the new market? We believe the balance of investors may change over time, so the initial patterns may not persist. There are a wide variety of potential investors, ranging from the individuals whose shares suddenly acquire a trading facility to sophisticated institutional investors. Whereas private investors represent only some 18% of the shareholdings (by value) in the Official List, we believe they may account for 25 or even 30% on AIM in the long term. This excludes the founder shareholders and directors – including them the proportion may be 40% or more.

16.1.1 Private investors

The number of private shareholders in the UK has grown from some 3 million in 1979 to a peak of 11 million in 1991 and fell to around 10 million at the end of 1993[1]. This growth has been fuelled by the privatisations of government monopolies. While 22% of the adult population in the UK are now shareholders, this is misleading to the extent that most of them own only those shares in privatised industries and have neither bought nor sold other shares. 51% of individual shareholders own shares in only one company; with only 21% holding shares in more than four companies. These latter figures lend support to the view that most of these individuals are passive holders of privatisation stocks and it is far from clear that the habit of risk taking through investment in shares has taken root.

The UK now compares favourably with other countries for individual shareholdings (see Table 16.1 below).

Country	*% of population*
UK	22%
France	13%
Germany	6%
Japan	9%
Switzerland	14%
USA	28%
Canada	23%

Table 16.1: Individual shareholders – percentage of adult population
Source: Proshare, quoted from report of Oesterreichische Kontrollbank Aktiengesellschaft, 1991

Despite the rise in individual shareholders in the UK, there is a continuing long-term decline in the percentage of the stock market owned by individuals and a rise in that owned by institutions. Figure 16.1 illustrates this dramatic fall in individual share ownership from nearly 70% of the market in 1953 to a mere 18% now. This process may be driven by tax advantages available to investment through the intermediation of institutions. It will not be helped by changes in settlement procedures that encourage the use of brokers nominee accounts since these currently block investors from receiving information directly from the companies in which they hold shares.

---

[1] Based on figures published by Proshare, produced by NOP and MORI.

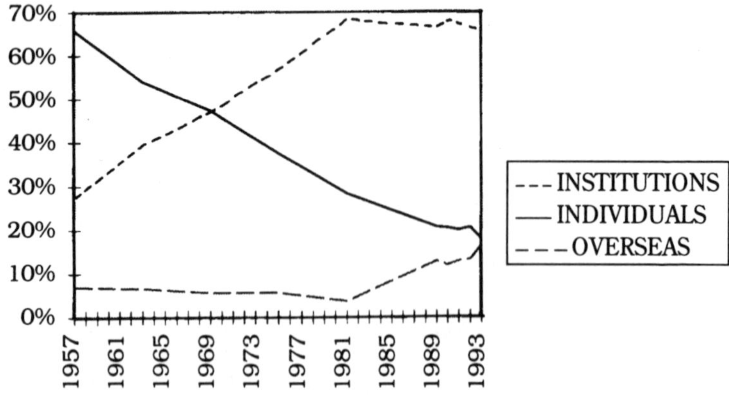

Figure 16.1: Percentage ownership of shares traded on the London Stock Exchange by investor type
Source: DTI

56% of individual shareholders are male and 40% live in the South East of England. The age range is a little broader than might have been imagined (see Table 16.2).

16–24	6%
25–39	25%
40–54	31%
55–64	19%
65+	19%

Table 16.2: Age range of individual shareholders
Source: NOP Survey for HM Treasury, 1993

The socio-economic distribution is also surprising in that, while biased towards those from professional and managerial backgrounds, it also includes considerable numbers from other backgrounds (see Table 16.3).

AB	33%
C1	29%
C2	23%
D/E	15%

Table 16.3: Socio-economic range of individual shareholders
Source: NOP Survey for HM Treasury, 1993

We believe there will be considerable long-term interest from private investors who will be attracted to AIM (as they were to BES) because of the tax reliefs available. They may also be attracted by the excitement of the market if the AIM management are able to create this mood and if there are some good inaugural issues. There would be a risk to this if there were an early spate of failures leading investors to become disenchanted with the market as a whole rather than just suspicious of the individual nominated advisers. However, on the other hand, directors of AIM companies should be reluctant to see the majority of their shares disappearing into the hands of tax driven investors, not to emerge for years and killing the aftermarket. A lack of share trading after a fund raising would remove one of the reasons for a trading facility in the first place. Not only do less liquid shares generally trade at a depressed multiple of earnings but further fund raising is likely to be impeded for this very reason. Directors will probably therefore seek a wide range of investors, including institutions.

Private investors will have to form their own judgement of the likely progress of companies traded on AIM. Some will move to a full listing in due course, losing the tax advantages of trading on AIM. Private investors may deal with this by concentrating on those companies that offer undertakings not to seek a full listing within a specified period. However it may be hard to get certainty. The AIM market might fail and be dissolved like the USM, so investors would need to know that the directors would seek the most appropriate alternative trading facility even at the cost of losing shareholders tax reliefs (see **16.2**).

A specific class of private investor that may be particularly interested in AIM is that body of people who belong to investment clubs. Brokers have observed a long-term growth, rather than just a cyclical recovery, in this sector. The 800 or 1,000 such clubs that exist in the UK probably represent an average of only 20 members, each investing a few hundred pounds a year, which translates into a total to cover all their investment activities of £5m to £10m per annum. While only a small proportion of this is likely to find its way into AIM, investors may also invest privately, outside the club itself. Such funding may be of particular relevance to smaller companies seeking to raise modest sums for expansion. This is also a source of investment of a local nature, since club members may be attracted to local companies they can physically visit, patronise or even just drive past.

16.1.2 Brokers' private clients

Some brokers could invest their discretionary managed funds on AIM, particularly to take advantage of tax reliefs for their clients. However the rules of the regulatory bodies require such clients to be introduced to suitable investments. The higher risk that may be associated with individual AIM shares and their lesser marketability compared with blue chip investments will restrict the number of investors for whom they are suitable. This may, therefore, encourage interest in specialist funds which are more easily able to spread their risk over a number of AIM securities.

In any case, this market is likely to be both finite and fairly small. Generally, the brokers can only expose their clients to a limited number of higher risk investments, although they would balance their risk better by having a wider spread of such higher risk investments. For non-discretionary funds there may be a more gradual build-up of interest as the market matures.

16.1.3 Institutional investors

Memory Corporation, a recent flotation on the 4.2 Market, has some £10 to £12m of shares at market value in public hands and has over 20 institutional shareholders as well as hundreds of private investors. This suggests that there are a large number of institutional investors who are involved in the 4.2 Market and are therefore likely to be interested in AIM. We believe that in mid-1995 there are at least 30, and perhaps as many as 50, institutions currently investing in 4.2 stocks. There is a specialist fund called Beacon Trust that raised £19m to invest in Rule 4.2 companies, Sime & Ivory have a smaller companies fund and we are aware of other managers working on developing funds in this area. It is quite clear, therefore, that there will be considerable institutional activity in AIM.

For some institutions, the size of AIM company will be an important issue for them. If one imagines a typical investing fund having £20m under management, then the costs of administration are likely to lead to its management wanting no more than 100 investments. This implies that the minimum institutional investment would be over £200,000 and that means that the investee company for institutional funds is likely to have a market capitalisation in excess of £2m. However, we have spoken to other institutions that are structured in such a way that they have no problem investing as little as £50,000 in a company.

Unit trusts are unlikely to be direct investors in AIM because the relatively small size of AIM companies may conflict with the trusts requirement to have no more than 5% invested in one company. The trust managers would also have to convince themselves and their trustees that AIM was an eligible market under the SIB regulations (particularly relating to liquidity). It will be far easier to invest in AIM indirectly through specialist funds quoted on the Official List. Similarly, we believe that Life Insurance Companies will invest in AIM indirectly, although AIM securities will be treated as listed for the calculation of their solvency ratio (DTI regulations proposed for September 1995).

There is a lot of evidence, before AIM has opened, that institutions are adopting an attitude of 'wait and see' rather than committing themselves to investing a certain proportion of their funds in smaller companies. They will want to see what quality of company is available for investment and how they perform.

The investing institutions will be excited by particular companies rather than just the mere fact of a new issue. They are attracted by:

- a reputable broker and adviser (if different);
- evidence of due diligence.

A number of institutional investors have expressed less interest in the formal due diligence carried out by accountants than in a commercial examination of the prospects for a market as well as for the specific company within it. In this context it is interesting that new issues on NASDAQ put more emphasis on such considerations of future prospects than has been customary in the UK.

16.2 TAX RELIEFS FOR INVESTORS

It has been announced that securities traded on AIM will be treated as unquoted by the Inland Revenue (IR Press Release 20 February 1995) for tax purposes. This will give an enormous boost to the new market, making it particularly attractive to three classes of shareholder:

- wealthy individuals who are able to make use of tax shelters;
- management shareholders;
- through the mechanism of Venture Capital Trusts and Enterprise Investment Schemes the tax reliefs will also provide benefit to many ordinary investors.

Clearly it would be unwise for a potential investor to put money into shares traded on AIM without considering that investments in this market are likely, on average, to present a higher risk than equities on the Official List. Indeed, as has been mentioned elsewhere, the further one gets from blue chip stocks the higher the risk. Without the ability to spread investment risk, an individual might save, say, a 20% tax bill at the cost of losing 100% of their money in a failed investment.

Investments in shares traded on AIM will qualify for the various tax reliefs available to unquoted securities, as described below.

16.2.1 Inheritance tax

Inheritance tax business property relief is available to the estates of investors in shares of companies traded on AIM (IHTA Part V, Chapter I). The relief is a 100% deduction against inheritance tax where the deceased owned 25% or more of the voting rights in a company and a 50% deduction for a lesser percentage holding.

The relief applies:

- where shares have been held for at least two years (or where they replace other assets that qualify and the combined period exceeds two years);
- for qualifying trades, ie excluding investment companies.

The relief is reduced to the extent that the company in which shares are held owned non-trading assets within the two years previous to the death of the investor.

This tax relief may provide a considerable encouragement to wealthy individuals to shelter their estates from inheritance tax. For example, an individual with a valuable holding (controlling in excess of 25% of the voting rights) in an AIM company and whose estate was liable to 40% tax on this, would be able to avoid the inheritance tax liability completely. A shareholding below the 25% threshold would be liable only to 20% inheritance tax.

16.2.2 Income tax relief

There is a tax benefit available to investors in being able to offset losses incurred on AIM investments against their income tax liability.

Relief for losses

Individuals are able to elect to claim tax relief for losses against their income tax rather than against capital gains tax (TA 1988 ss 573–576). This applies only where the investor has subscribed for the shares in the primary issue and not where they buy them in the market. This is particularly helpful if the investor has no capital gains against which to offset losses they may have incurred on investments. The key features are:

1 *Occurrence of loss* – the loss occurs when:
   (a) the individual sells shares for less than they paid for them; or
   (b) a company goes into liquidation (the shareholders of a company being liquidated will receive notification from the liquidator which will give the relevant date and the amount of any distribution to shareholders); or
   (c) the shares can be shown to have negligible value.

   The loss is the same as would be computed for capital gains tax purposes. It is not, however, possible to use the annual indexation allowance to increase the loss for tax purposes.

2 *Qualifying trading company* – the shares must be ordinary shares in a 'qualifying trading company' which is defined as one that:
   (a) is a UK resident trading company; or
   (b) is the UK resident holding company for a trading group; or
   (c) ceased to be a UK trading company within the previous three years.

The principal activity of the company must not be dealing in securities, loans, trade or commodity futures. If it has been such an 'excluded company' or has been an investment company then a period of six years must have elapsed during which it has been a trading company.

3 *Procedure*: the individual must make a claim in writing within two years after the end of the year of assessment in which the loss or losses occur.
4 *Carry back*: as with other loss relief against income taxes, any unrelieved losses can be carried back to the preceding year of assessment.

16.2.3 Capital gains tax

There are two tax reliefs available against capital gains tax liabilities: reinvestment relief and holdover relief (TCGA 1992 s 164A–N).

Reinvestment relief

An individual (or a trust whose beneficiaries are individuals) who realises a taxable gain, may defer paying all or some of the tax due on the gain. A sum up to the amount of the gain can be invested in unquoted securities, which includes shares traded on AIM. The tax is then not payable until these shares are sold, and the purchase of further shares, further postpones payment. The investment in shares must take place within a period starting twelve months before the gain is realised and finishing three years afterwards. Any gains – with no maximum or minimum limits – that have occurred after 30th November 1993 are eligible.

Since the purpose of this relief is to encourage investment in unquoted trading companies, there must be no arrangements in place before shares are purchased for them to be sold in the future. This is to prevent the relief applying to transactions that are really loans subsidised by the taxpayer. Examples include the many property based Business Enterprise Schemes where the shareholder bought shares, obtained tax relief and had an arrangement to sell the shares back to the 'borrower' at a specified time in the future. Similarly, the shareholder must not receive excessive value in the form of dividends, remuneration etc.

To obtain this tax relief, the individual must acquire 'eligible' shares, which are ordinary shares, carrying no preferential rights to income or capital. The shares must be in a 'qualifying' company which is:

1 An unquoted trading company or an unquoted holding company with subsidiaries which are trading companies.

2 Not engaged to a substantial extent in:
   (a) dealing in land, commodities or shares;
   (b) dealing in goods other than in the ordinary course of manufacture or distribution;
   (c) financial services;
   (d) legal or accountancy services;
   (e) provision of services to a connected company which is a non-qualifying company.

An individual may claim this relief even if they take an active role in the management of the company they invest in, so they may also be eligible for retirement relief.

Holdover relief

This particular tax relief is available to encourage entrepreneurs to pass down business assets to their children (TCGA 1992 ss 1, 165–169). Normally, when assets are disposed of and it is not an arms length transaction then market value must be substituted for any price actually paid. This may result in a capital gain arising and therefore a tax liability. A gift of business assets to a son or daughter may therefore give rise to a capital gains tax liability immediately, as well as a potential inheritance tax liability.

If the asset is a 'business asset' then the tax liability can be postponed. Suppose, for example, that a mother gave a business asset with a market value of £100,000 to her child while the original cost (adjusted for indexation allowance) was £60,000. In normal circumstances, the mother would have a liability for tax on £40,000 (£100,000 less £60,000). However, by making an election this can be deferred until the asset is sold by the child. When that happens the assumed cost, for calculating any tax liability, is the original cost to the mother of £60,000.

Investments in companies whose shares are traded on AIM will qualify for this relief subject to the following:

1 The shareholding must amount to at least 5% of the voting rights.
2 The business of the company or, if it is a holding company, of its subsidiaries must be trading.

3 If the company owns assets that are not used in its trade then the relief is restricted. This is intended to ensure that property holding and finance companies do not benefit from the relief.
4 The individual making the election must be ordinarily resident in the UK.

The relief is not intended to attract foreigners who merely seek to establish a UK tax shelter. Nonetheless there is a period of grace for those leaving the UK temporarily.

16.2.4 Combined relief

The greatest benefits arise when a combination of tax reliefs can be claimed on unquoted investments and this occurs with the schemes outlined below (FA 1994 s 137 and Sch 15).

Enterprise Investment Scheme

The Enterprise Investment Scheme (EIS) is the replacement of the Business Expansion Scheme (BES). It gives a 20% tax credit to individuals investing in 'eligible shares in qualifying companies'. The definitions of eligible and qualifying are as given above (see **16.2.3**) for reinvestment relief. In addition, the investment is exempt from capital gains tax once it has been held for at least five years. If shares are sold within five years or if the company ceases to be eligible then the 20% EIS relief is clawed back. If shares are sold within five years and a loss results to the investor then there is additional tax relief available so that an investor paying higher rate tax would get total relief at 40% for the loss but would not get the 20% EIS credit on top of that.

Individuals may claim relief for investments of up to £100,000 in any tax year and companies may raise funds from EIS investors with an aggregate value of up to £1m in any tax year. Individuals, together with their immediate family and business associates, are restricted to a 30% holding in an eligible company.

EIS relief is available to individuals who were previously unconnected but become paid directors of the company they are investing in.

The company whose shares are invested in must not become 'ineligible', as defined under the section on reinvestment relief, for three years after the date of investment (or the date trading commences if that is later). If the company does become ineligible then the EIS relief is clawed back and capital gains tax is due on any subsequent sale which shows a profit.

Venture Capital Trusts

The Venture Capital Trust (VCT) was proposed in the 1994 Budget and legislation contained in the Finance Bill (Finance Act 1995 Schs 14 to 16). At the time of writing, the Finance Bill has not passed all of its parliamentary stages. In addition, much of the regulation of VCTs will be established by regulations to be issued by the government.

VCTs are to be companies whose income principally derives from investments in unquoted companies and, as long as they observe certain requirements and restrictions, they will confer certain tax advantages on their investors. Since AIM companies are to be treated as unquoted for tax purposes, the VCTs are likely to be natural investors in them. Because of other restrictions outlined below, where VCTs are investors, they are likely to invest primarily in smaller AIM companies.

While most of the conditions of obtaining tax reliefs are within the control of the VCT, there are a number which will have implications for the companies they invest in. It is likely that the VCT will seek assurances and possibly binding undertakings to ensure that the conditions continue to be observed. The principal conditions that must pertain in any accounting period are as follows:

1 The VCT's ordinary shares to be listed on the Stock Exchange (within two to three years of raising funds).
2 The VCT must not have retained more than 15% of its income from shares and securities.
3 That no holding (other than in another VCT) represents more than 15% of the value of its total investments.
4 That at least 70% by value of the investments of the VCT has been represented, throughout the period, by shares or loans in qualifying holdings. These are investments:

(a) of up to £1m. Any number of VCTs can invest at the same time, allowing the trading company to raise £10m – see (b) below for the explanation of this upper limit;
(b) in a company with gross assets (excluding liabilities) of up to £10m at the time the investment is made. There seems to be no reason why the trading company could not raise money above this limit, after the VCTs have completed their investment;
(c) that are subscribed by the VCT not purchased;
(d) in unquoted companies;
(e) in companies carrying on a qualifying trade which is not
   - dealing in land, commodities or financial instruments
   - dealing in goods other than of an ordinary trade of wholesale or retail distribution
   - banking, insurance or other financial services
   - receiving royalties or licence fees
   - legal or accountancy services;

(f) where the funds raised are not to finance a subsidiary outside the UK;
(g) where the VCT does not have control of the company.

The 70% test does not have to be satisfied at the outset but must be satisfied by an accounting period commencing within three years of approval of the VCT.

If the investment by a VCT is in a holding company, then all its subsidiaries must carry out a qualifying trade. This means that any minor non-qualifying trade should be carried out by a division and not by a subsidiary.

5 That at least 50% (by value) of the VCT's qualifying holdings are in the form of ordinary shares with no preferential rights. This 50% test does not have to be satisfied at the outset but must be satisfied by an accounting period commencing within three years of approval of the VCT.

The following tax reliefs will be available to individual investors (not companies) of up to £100,000 in any tax year:

1 Subscribers for new ordinary shares in VCTs will obtain income tax relief of 20% – as long as the shares are held for at least five years.
2 Investors (those who have bought in the market, not just subscribers for new shares) will be exempt from income tax on dividends and capital gains tax on disposals.

3 Subscribers will be able to defer payment of capital gains tax that is due from the disposal of any asset, as long as the gain is reinvested in VCTs.

In addition to the reliefs for individual investors, VCTs themselves will be exempt from corporation tax on capital gains.

Personal Equity Plans

AIM securities will not be eligible for individual investors' Personal Equity Plans (PEPs). This arises because investments included in a PEP must be quoted for tax purposes. There are representations being made to the Treasury to change this situation and to permit PEPs to include AIM stocks since that would further stimulate the market.

A particular problem arises for those individuals who have shares in USM companies within their PEPs. If the directors of those companies decide to move to AIM rather than to the Official List then the shares immediately become ineligible. They can be sold and the proceeds reinvested within the PEP or they can be transferred out of the fund to the investor. In this latter case, the value cannot be made up by further investment into the PEP except through the usual annual investment.

16.2.5 Other issues

Management shareholders

Directors who are also shareholders will be able to retain tax reliefs available for unquoted investments and this will be a particular attraction of AIM. It is quite possible that directors of smaller companies currently on the Official List may consider moving to AIM in order to take advantage of the tax reliefs, despite the effect this may have on their perceived status. If AIM develops as a respected alternative to the Official List then such a move might be very attractive to the many companies on the Official List which have limited trading in their shares. The tax reliefs of particular interest to directors will be:

1 Inheritance tax, where up to three director shareholders could all obtain 100% relief while still having over 20% of the shares in their business traded on AIM.
2 Holdover relief, where a director could transfer shares to a child or to a discretionary trust and still avoid a capital gains tax liability.
   (Note that the inheritance and capital gains tax reliefs can both be obtained for the same investment.)
3 EIS, where the director shareholders could obtain the relief and then raise additional finance through AIM while retaining their EIS benefits.

These reliefs will generally not apply to family trusts but only to individuals.

Comparison with the USM and Official List

Shareholdings in USM companies are also eligible for a number of tax reliefs. These include:

- business property relief for inheritance tax purposes;
- income tax relief for losses sustained on subscription for shares;
- purchase or redemption of a company's own shares treated as a disposal for capital gains tax purposes.

In addition, USM and Listed shares are eligible for inclusion in a PEP. Note that the USM will close at the end of 1996.

The interest on loans taken out to purchase shares is eligible for tax relief regardless of the market they trade through. This is available for close companies where the investor has a share stake in excess of 5%. A close company is one controlled (ie more than 50% of the voting rights) by no more than five shareholders.

Glossary

AIM	The Alternative Investment Market
Allotment	The procedure whereby a person becomes entitled to new securities, usually evidenced by an allotment letter which may be renounced in favour of someone else
AMEX	The American Exchange is the third largest US stock exchange by market capitalisation and is based in New York
Beneficial owner	The true owner of a security who receives the benefits arising from it
Best advantage	The duty of a member firm to deal at the best price for their client in all the circumstances of timing, deal size etc
Big Bang	In 1987 new rules were introduced by the London Stock Exchange. This abolished the separation of share dealings with the public from trading shares through the Exchange, previously carried out by brokers and jobbers respectively. This system was known as dual capacity. Allowing the same firms to carry out both functions led to much more highly capitalised firms forming and to banking institutions entering the market directly. For the first time commissions could be

	negotiated. This package of changes became known as Big Bang
Blue chip	This term is applied to the most highly regarded shares giving stable earnings in the largest companies. It derives from American gambling parlance where a blue chip was the one with the highest value
Broker	A member of the London Stock Exchange, providing dealing services to the public and possibly advice. A broker may also trade on its own account
Connected persons	Defined in s 346 of the Companies Act 1985. It broadly refers to family, friends and business associates
Consideration	Consideration is money or moneys worth paid in settlement of a contract
Continuous market	The continuous availability of bid and offer prices during the mandatory quote period
CREST	The Bank of England sponsored system that replaced the Exchange's Taurus project to provide paperless share registration and transfers. It is intended to be an optional system rather than being universal and compulsory
Earnings per share	A company's published earnings attributable to Ordinary Shareholders divided by the number of Ordinary Shares in issue
EASDAQ	A proposed European version of NASDAQ. A computer based stock exchange
Equity	The risk sharing portion of the company's capital that participates in income and capital
Exchange	The London International Stock Exchange of the United Kingdom and the Republic of Ireland which trades as The London Stock Exchange
False market	A false market exists when some investors or market makers have access to information that

is not generally available. Other investors are therefore making investment decisions based on false information

Flotation	Flotation is a term referring to the first admission of a security to trading on a stock exchange
Free float	The shares in a company that are not held by the company's directors, employees, connected persons and associated investors
FTSE Index	The Financial Times/Stock Exchange Index. There are a number of these indices, sponsored by these two institutions, which track the level of share prices through a historical series covering many years
Gilts	Government loan securities which pay a rate of interest and are generally redeemable at their original issue price on a fixed date
Global Depositary Receipt (GDR)	A negotiable certificate evidencing the ownership of securities lodged with an institution
Initial Public Offering (IPO)	The first offer for sale of shares to the public is an IPO. However the term 'public' is used to include investment institutions as well. An IPO may therefore be a placing as well as a public offer for sale.
Insider dealing	Buying or selling securities or financial instruments based on the value of securities while having access to information about changes in their value that is not generally available
Internet	A series of communication protocols which allow computers worldwide to send messages to each other. This has grown with the practice of organisations allowing open or restricted access to data on their computers and with the development of intermediaries who can provide access to long distance

	telephone lines for the cost of a local telephone call
Issuer	An incorporated body which issues securities that are currently, or will be, traded on AIM
Listed company	A company whose shares are traded on the main London Stock Exchange and whose share transactions are included in the Daily Official List
Listing particulars	Admission to the Official List of the London Stock Exchange requires the production of a document called listing particulars carrying detailed information that is additional to the prospectus. The information to be included in this is detailed in a publication of the Exchange, often called the Yellow Book
Mandatory quote period	Between 8.30 am and 4.30 pm. Between these times particular rules apply to the dealing of market makers. The time period is different on different country sections of SEAQ International
Market maker	A market maker who is registered in a security, trades them on a buy or sell basis, taking a dealing profit from the difference between the two prices
Matched bargain	A matched bargain occurs when a broker finds someone who wants to buy a security to trade with a willing seller or vice versa
Mid-market price	The average of the buying and selling price
NASDAQ	National Association of Securities Dealers Automated Quote. This is the second largest US stock exchange by market capitalisation. It is often viewed as a market for smaller, growing companies
Nominee	A name in which a security is registered, held in trust for the beneficial owner

Normal market size (NMS)	A calculation of a notional 'normal' institutional bargain in a security. This is taken as the total share turnover in the previous year, divided by a notional 250 trading days and then multiplied by 2.5%. The resulting figure is placed within one of 12 bands. The NMS is the minimum size of bargain for which market makers may quote a price
NYSE	The New York Stock Exchange is the largest US stock exchange capitalised at some £2.7 bn at the end of 1994
Official List	The Official List of the London Stock Exchange is a daily list of share dealings (giving the transaction price) settled through the Exchange's Talisman system
Ordinary shares	Units of the equity of a company, all having equal value and status. Ordinary shares participate without limit in the capital and earnings of the company
Parent undertaking	A parent controls the majority of the voting rights or the power to appoint the majority of the board or exercises a dominant influence – see s 258 Companies Act 1985
Personal Equity Plan (PEP)	A UK tax scheme allowing shares owned by individuals to be put into a tax exempt fund
Placing	The issue of new securities through a sale to investing institutions via an intermediary. The placees may, in turn, sell on the securities to clients or to investment funds under their control
POS Regulations	Public Offer of Securities Regulations 1995 – published by HM Treasury. The authority for these regulations is the Financial Services Act 1986. They apply only to securities offered to the public in the UK

Preliminary announcement	It has become customary to issue a formal announcement of annual and interim financial results through the Exchange when they are agreed with the auditors. The printed report and accounts are then sent out two to three weeks later
Price Earnings Ratio	The current share price divided by the last published annual earnings per share
Prospectus	A prospectus is a document issued to potential investors to provide them with information necessary to make an informed investment decision. The information to be included is covered by statute. See Public Offer of Securities Regulations 1995 – published by HM Treasury
Public Limited Company	A UK limited company that is permitted by law to issue securities to the public
Registrar	A company registrar is a company retained to manage another company's share register. Many of the banks have subsidiaries that perform this service
Regulatory News Service (RNS)	The Stock Exchange's news service for disseminating price sensitive information about companies. This is primarily achieved through electronic messages via SEAQ
Rights issue	An invitation to existing shareholders to subscribe for new shares pro rata to their existing holding
Scrip issue	The issue of new shares to existing shareholders pro rata to their existing holding. This is generally done without consideration in order to reduce the price of shares trading at several pounds each, or to effect a capital reconstruction. A tax avoidance scheme, known as enhanced scrip dividends, has also been used whereby shares are issued in place of dividends

SEAQ	The Stock Exchange Automated Quotations System. This is a computer database containing prices quoted by market makers and details of trades completed
Secondary market	The term has no precise definition but relates to a second tier market, separate from the main official stock exchange but under its auspices. Generally, the securities of younger and smaller companies will be traded
Securities and Futures Authority	One of the self regulating organisations established under the Financial Services Act 1986 to regulate the provision of investment services to the public
Securities and Investment Board	An agency of HM Treasury empowered under the Financial Services Act 1986 to regulate and to delegate the regulation of investment business
SEDOL	The Stock Exchange Daily Official List. It is the unique number given to each company traded through the Exchange
SEPON	Stock Exchange Pool Nominees Ltd is the entity used by the Exchange as an intermediate stage in executing share transfers through its Talisman settlement system
Settlement	The process, following a trade, of transferring share ownership from a seller to a buyer accompanied by the buyer paying the seller for them
Shadow director	A shadow director is defined in s 741 Companies Act 1985. A person whose instructions are customarily followed by employees or staff of a company. Under certain circumstances they are treated, by the law, as directors of the company
Spread	(i) The difference between one market maker's bid and offer prices

	(ii) An expression relating to the degree of dispersion of securities among different investors
Subsidiary undertaking	See parent undertaking and s 258 and s 736 Companies Act 1985
Talisman	The automated settlement system of the London Stock Exchange
Taurus	The Stock Exchange's proposed system for recording share ownership and transactions, intended to supersede paper share certificates. The project was abandoned in 1992 and replaced by CREST – sponsored by the Bank of England
TOPIC	Formerly the system whereby the Exchange disseminated information on shares to subscribers. This is now largely done by independent information vendors who get their information by direct link from the Exchange
Touch	The best buying and selling prices of a security available at any time from a market maker through SEAQ
Underwriting	A contract entered into by an offeror of securities with an underwriter, whereby the latter undertakes to buy all the securities not sold to the public by way of an offer for sale
Venture capital	Finance provided by investors to assist development of a company in return for an equity stake. The term usually refers to finance provided by specialist institutional investors to companies that are not yet large enough to have their shares traded through an exchange
Warrant	A security giving the holder the right to subscribe for securities at a prescribed price at a future date

Appendices

Appendix 1

Nominated advisers application form – NA1

London STOCK EXCHANGE

1. Name of applicant:

Trading name (if different):

Address:

Postcode:

Tel: | Fax: | STX:

2. Nature of entity (limited company, unlimited company, partnership):

If a body corporate, country of incorporation:

3. Name of contact:

4. Is the applicant:
i Authorised under the Financial Services Act 1986? Yes No

Please indicate any self regulating organisation(s) or recognised professional body of which the applicant is a member:

If appropriate, state the applicant's lead regulator:

ii A member of the London Stock Exchange Yes No

5. Has the applicant been operating in a principal corporate finance advisory role for at least the last three years? Yes No

ID: 2.1568

6. Describe completed initial public offers, demergers, or other issues of securities involving listing particulars, USM particulars, a Companies Act prospectus or equivalent EU documents or other appropriate major transactions involving listed or other public companies, in which the applicant has acted in a principal corporate finance advisory role within the last three years*:

Transaction:	Experience:	Date:

*Continue on a separate sheet where necessary

2

7. Name at least four suitably qualified and experienced executive staff, as defined in the Nominated Advisers Eligibility Criteria as published by the Exchange from time to time.

Title	First name	Surname

8. State the number of staff who will be involved in an executive capacity in nominated adviser activities:

9. What procedures and controls are in place to ensure that personnel do not act beyond their proper authority?

Note: Copies of procedures may be requested during the application process.

10. Is there any other information which you think may be relevant to the Exchange in considering this application? Yes No

If the answer is yes, give details on a separate sheet.

3

11. Nominated adviser's undertaking to the London Stock Exchange (to be signed by all applicants)

Name of nominated adviser

hereby applies for approval as a nominated adviser for the purpose of the AIM Admission Rules and if you grant this application undertakes to:

- i discharge its responsibilities as a nominated adviser under the AIM Admission Rules from time to time
- ii advise you in writing without delay if:
  - a it ceases to be an authorised person as required by Rule 16.28 of the AIM Admission Rules
  - b it is the subject of an intervention order or any disciplinary proceedings or similar action by any regulator under the Financial Services Act 1986 or under any comparable legislation in any member state outside the United Kingdom
- iii advise you without delay of any change to the staff who are involved in an executive capacity in nominated adviser activities, including details of the qualifications and experience of any new staff to be involved in an executive capacity in nominated adviser activities
- iv advise you in writing without delay of its resignation or dismissal, giving details of any relevant facts or circumstances
- v perform the role of nominated adviser only for any organisation from which it is independent as defined in the eligibility criteria as published by the Exchange from time to time
- vi continue to comply with the eligibility criteria

and acknowledges that:

- vii you may censure it and/or remove its name from the register of nominated advisers maintained by you if:
  - a you consider that it is in breach of its responsibilities
  - b you consider that the integrity and reputation of the market may have been impaired as a result of its conduct or judgement; or
  - c the number of suitably qualified and experienced executive staff in its employ falls below four

and that you may publicise the fact that you have done so and the reasons for your action

- viii appeals to the AIM Appeals Committee will be dealt with in accordance with the AIM Appeals Procedures as published from time to time.

We declare that the information supplied is complete and correct and agree to comply with the additional notification requirements.

We have read the Nominated Advisers Eligibility Criteria and framework for making applications and believe that this application conforms to the criteria (except as specifically notified to you with this application).

This undertaking must be signed by two directors, partners or duly authorised officers of the nominated adviser.

Signed:	Date:
Name of signatory in block capitals:	
Partner, director or duly authorised officer, for and on behalf of (name of nominated adviser):	

Signed:	Date:
Name of signatory in block capitals:	
Partner/director or duly authorised officer, for and on behalf of (name of nominated adviser):	

Please return this form to:
AIM
London Stock Exchange
London EC2N 1HP

4

Appendix to nominated advisers form NA1

1. Name of applicant:

2. Give details of executive staff who will be involved in nominated adviser activities*.

In the examination column enter the appropriate number as follows:

i the individual has passed, been exempted or grandfathered from the SFA's Corporate Finance Representative Examination or General/Securities Representative Examination

ii the individual is applying for a waiver from the nominated adviser examination requirements. **Form NA3 must be attached in such cases.**

iii the individual has already been granted a waiver from the nominated adviser examination requirements

All Form NA2s must be submitted at the time of application or as soon as possible thereafter. Delay in sending the forms will lead to delay in the handling of the application.

If any of the executive staff involved in nominated adviser activities are seeking to have the examination requirement waived, attach Form NA3 in addition to Form NA2.

Title:	First name(s):	Surname:	Examination:	Form NA2 attached:	
				Yes	No
				Yes	No
				Yes	No
				Yes	No
				Yes	No
				Yes	No
				Yes	No
				Yes	No
				Yes	No
				Yes	No
				Yes	No
				Yes	No
				Yes	No
				Yes	No
				Yes	No

*Continue on a separate sheet where necessary

5

Appendix 2

Nominated adviser employee form – NA2

London **STOCK EXCHANGE**

This form is to be completed when:

A An initial application is submitted by a nominated adviser applicant

B An executive staff member who has not previously been involved in nominated adviser activities joins an existing nominated adviser; or

C An executive staff member is to be named by a nominated adviser as being suitably qualified and experienced, as defined in the Nominated Advisers Eligibility Criteria as published by the London Stock Exchange from time to time.

1. Personal details:

Name of nominated adviser applicant:

2. Executive staff member's full name:

Title: First name(s):

Surname: Date of birth:

3. Private address:

Postcode:

4. Qualifications:
Provide details of any professional or business qualifications and/or memberships of any professional bodies, exchanges or trade associations obtained or applied for.*

5. Have you passed, been grandfathered into, exempted or received a waiver from the SFA RP5 or General/Securities Representatives Examination? Yes No

If yes, which?

If no, are you applying for a waiver from the examination requirements for executive staff involved in nominated adviser activities ? Yes No

If yes, attach completed form NA3 and fee if appropriate.

*Continue answers on a separate sheet where necessary

ID: 2 1566

1

6. Employment history
Provide details of your employment history (last 10 years, most recent first)*:

Dates from/to:	Name and address of organisation:	Position held/responsibilities:

7. Transaction history
Describe completed initial public offers, demergers, or other issues of securities involving listing particulars, USM particulars, a Companies Act prospectus or equivalent EU documents or other appropriate major transactions involving listed or other public companies in which the nominated adviser applicant has acted in a principal corporate finance advisory role within the last three years and in which you have had direct experience. If this includes equivalent experience gained whilst working for a previous employer, this fact must be indicated*.

Transaction:	Experience:	Date:

8. Declaration
I declare that the information supplied is complete and correct.

Signature:	Date:
Name of signatory in block capitals:	

*Continue answers on a separate sheet where necessary

Please return this form to:
AIM
London Stock Exchange
London EC2N 1HP

2

Appendix 3

Nominated advisers
Examination waiver
application form – NA3

London STOCK EXCHANGE

Application for waiver of examination requirements

Name:

Date of birth:

Name of applicant:

Category of waiver applied for:

Notes

There are three categories of waiver:

Category A applies where an individual has reasonably continuous relevant corporate finance experience since 1 January 1986. To demonstrate 'relevant experience' an individual must have been involved in an executive capacity in giving corporate finance advice, including having direct contact with client companies and/or the London Stock Exchange.

Category A applicants must complete questions 1 and 2 and the declaration.

Category B applies where an individual has had three years' recent and reasonably continuous experience in giving relevant corporate finance advice and holds one of the following:

i qualifications of a barrister, advocate or solicitor who has been called or admitted in any part of the UK

ii qualifications for appointment as an auditor, accountant or public company secretary in the UK

iii membership of the Securities Institute.

Category B applicants must complete questions 1 and 2 and the declaration.

Category C applies where other individuals seek a waiver by virtue of the breadth of their experience in giving corporate finance advice. Very few applications are expected to be granted under category C.

Category C applicants must complete questions 1 and 3 and the declaration.

ID: 2.1568

1. (All applicants)

Describe your corporate finance experience since 1 January 1986. State in the direct contact column if you had direct contact with client companies and/or the Exchange.

Date: (month and year)	Employer:	Job title and major responsibilities:	Direct contact:

2. (Category A and B applicants)

Do you have one of the following:

i qualifications of a barrister, advocate or solicitor who has been called or admitted in any part of the UK? Yes No

ii qualifications of an auditor, accountant or public company secretary in the UK? Yes No

iii membership of the Securities Institute? Yes No

If yes, **provide documentary evidence**. If you have answered yes to more than one, you need only provide documentary evidence for one of the above.

2

3. (Category C applicants only)

Describe your corporate finance experience and your justification for seeking an exceptional waiver*:

*Continue on a separate sheet if necessary

Declaration (All applicants)

I declare that the information supplied is complete and correct.

I understand that the information may be verified in such manner as the Exchange may decide.

I attach (**Category B** applicants only) documentary evidence of qualifications/Securities Institute membership ☐ (tick if appropriate)

Signature:	Date:

Please return this form to:
AIM
London Stock Exchange
London EC2N 1HP

3

Appendix 4

London STOCK EXCHANGE

Declaration by the nominated adviser

To: AIM
London Stock Exchange
London EC2N 1HP

__________19__

Full name of nominated adviser:

Full name of issuer and details of the securities to which this declaration applies:

Type of issue for which application for admission to trading on AIM is being made (indicate if not appropriate):

I, ______________________________ a partner/director of the above nominated adviser, or an officer duly authorised to give this declaration, hereby confirm

a that, in relation to the application for admission:

i the directors of the issuer have received advice and guidance (from this firm or other appropriate professional adviser) as to the nature of their responsibilities and obligations to ensure compliance by the issuer with the AIM Admission Rules in Chapter 16 of the Rules of the London Stock Exchange as amended from time to time

ii to the best of my knowledge and belief, all relevant requirements of the AIM Admission Rules (save for the admission document's compliance with Regulation 9 of the Public Offers of Securities Regulations 1995) have been complied with:

(The statements in paragraph a are applicable only if this application relates to an issue of securities requiring the publication of an admission document. Delete if inappropriate)

b that this firm will be available at all times to advise and guide the directors of the issuer as to their responsibilities and obligations to ensure compliance by the issuer on an ongoing basis with the AIM Admission Rules;

c that this firm will comply with the AIM Admission Rules applicable to it in its role as nominated adviser; and

d that this firm will confirm to the Exchange in writing when it ceases to be the issuer's nominated adviser.

Signed:

Partner/director or duly authorised officer, for and on behalf of
Name of nominated adviser:

Admission to AIM expected on: ____________________19__

Name(s) of contact(s) at nominated adviser regarding the application:

Telephone/STX number:

Appendix 5

London STOCK EXCHANGE

Application to be signed by the company

To: AIM
London Stock Exchange
London EC2N 1HP

__________19__

Name of issuer of the securities:

('The issuer')

hereby applies for the securities detailed below to be admitted for trading on AIM subject to the Rules of the London Stock Exchange.

Details of securities to be admitted to trading on AIM

Amounts and descriptions of securities for which application is now being made:

Admission to AIM expected on: ________________19__

Name(s) of contact(s) at issuer regarding the application:

Telephone number:

Declaration

i The directors of the issuer have received advice and guidance (from the nominated adviser or other appropriate professional adviser) as to the nature of their responsibilities and obligations to ensure compliance by the issuer with the AIM Admission Rules in Chapter 16 of the Rules of the London Stock Exchange as amended from time to time and fully understand and accept these responsibilities and obligations

ii the issuer has taken appropriate advice where necessary and has acted appropriately on any advice given

iii the admission document complies with the AIM Admission Rules and includes all such information as investors would reasonably require, and reasonably expect to find there, for the purpose of making an informed assessment of the assets and liabilities, financial position, profits and losses, and prospects of the issuer of the securities and the rights attaching to those securities

iv in the opinion of the issuer, having made due and careful enquiry, the working capital available to the issuer and its group is sufficient for their present requirements

v any profit forecast, estimate or projection in the admission document has been made after due and careful enquiry by the issuer; and

vi procedures have been established which provide a reasonable basis for the directors to make proper judgements as to the financial position and prospects of the issuer and its group.

Undertaking

We undertake to:

i comply with the AIM Admission Rules set out in Chapter 16 of the Rules of the London Stock Exchange as amended from time to time by the Exchange; and

ii seek advice and guidance from the nominated adviser when appropriate and act appropriately on such advice.

Signed:

Director, secretary or other duly authorised officer for and on behalf of
Name of the issuer:

Note: paragraphs (iii) to (v) of the Declaration are applicable only if this application relates to an issue of securities requiring the publication of an admission document. Delete if appropriate.

Appendix 6

CISCO (THE CITY GROUP FOR SMALLER COMPANIES) RECOMMENDATIONS FOR MATTERS WHICH SHOULD BE PRESENTED TO THE BOARD

Management structure and senior management responsibilities.

Nomination of directors.

Appointment of chairman.

Appointment of managing director.

Appointment or removal of company secretary.

Senior management appointments.

Remuneration, contracts and grants of options for senior management.

Business strategy.

Operating budgets.

Diversification/retrenchment policy.

Acquisitions and disposals of subsidiaries or other liabilities over, say, 5% of net assets/profits.

Investments and capital projects over a similar level.

Other transactions over a similar level.

Substantial commitments including:

- pension funding
- contracts in excess of one year's duration

- giving of security over significant group assets *(incuding mortgages and charges over the company's property)*

Contracts not in the ordinary course of business.

Raising new capital and confirmation of major financing facilities.

Treasury policies including foreign currency and interest rate exposure.

Specific risk management policies including insurance, hedging, borrowing limits, corporate security.

Agreement of code of ethics and business practice.

Establishment of overall framework for proper control eg internal audit.

Establishment of managerial authority limit for smaller transactions.

Actions or transactions where there may be doubt over their legality or propriety.

Agreeing membership and terms of reference of board committees and task forces.

Matters referred to the board by board committees.

Governance of company pension schemes and appointment of company nominees to board of trustees.

Final approval of annual and interim reports and accounts and accounting policies.

Appointment/proposal of auditors.

Approval of prospectuses, issue documents.

Approval and recommendation of dividends.

Allotment, calls or forfeiture of shares.

Disclosure of director's interests.

Avoidance of wrongful or fraudulent trading.

Calling of shareholders' meetings.

Delegation of the board's powers.

Authorising use of company seal.

Charitable and political donations.

Appendix 7

EXAMPLES OF SERVICES PROVIDED BY COMPANY REGISTRARS

A company registrar assists the company secretary with day-to-day administration of the share register, which may be particularly valuable when substantial numbers of share transfers take place in securities or where new capital issues occur. They can cover a wide variety of separate services:

- maintaining and updating the register of members, for example dealing with changes of address;
- registering and certifying share transfers;
- preparing sealing and despatching share certificates;
- processing dividend payments and reconciling bank statements, for example as well as conventional dividends they could administer scrip dividends or dividend reinvestment schemes;
- preparing labels and sending out annual reports, interim statements and other circulars to shareholders;
- administering share issues, for example for rights issues; calculating entitlements, sending circulars, collating responses, amending the share register, issuing certificates etc;
- administration of polls required for shareholders meetings, for example checking proxy cards;
- analysis of shareholders, for example listings of major shareholders, tracking of changes in nominee accounts. They may be able to

provide enquiry facilities through on-line computer links or regular despatch of up-dated computer discs;

- sending and administering s 212 notices.

The registrar may also, through trustee schemes, administer employee share schemes such as profit sharing schemes, executive share options, savings-related share option schemes etc.

They may also offer general company secretarial services.

Appendix 8

FURTHER READING

Documents published by the London Stock Exchange

AIM – Changes to the Rules of the London Stock Exchange (February 1995, revised June 1995)

The AIM Appeals Procedures (June 1995)

Guidance on the dissemination of price sensitive information (February 1995)

Nominated advisers – Eligibility criteria and framework for making applications

AIM Register of nominated advisers (June 1995)

UK Securities Industry Equity Settlement – Code of Good Practice (December 1994)

Regulatory News Service Procedural Guidelines (August 1994)

Stock Exchange Alternative Trading Service User Guide (1993)

Explanatory booklets

A guide for advisers and brokers (February 1995)
A guide for companies (February 1995)
A guide for investors (February 1995)
Notice N16/95 – Transitional Arrangements

Other publications

Public Offer of Securities Regulations 1995, HMSO, June 1995

The Financial Services Act 1986 (Investment Advertisement) (Exemptions) (No 2) Order 1995

The Financial Aspects of Corporate Governance (Guidance for Smaller Companies), City Group for Smaller Companies, 1993

Financial Reporting Standard 4 'Capital Instruments', Accounting Standards Board, December 1993

Auditing Guideline: Prospectuses & the Reporting Accountant.

Index

Index entries with full points refer to numbered headings. Those without full points refer to page numbers.